becoming designers

education & influence

edited by **Esther Dudley & Stuart Mealing**

COLLEGE OF RIPON
AND YORK ST JOHN
LIBRARY

intellect™
EXETER, ENGLAND

College of Ripon & York St. John

3 8025 00391729 4

D1638959

First Published in Paperback in 2000 by
Intellect Books, FAE, Earl Richards Road North, Exeter EX2 6AS, UK

First Published in USA in 2000 by
Intellect Books, ISBS, 5804 N.E. Hassalo St, Portland, Oregon 97213-3644, USA

Copyright ©2000 Intellect Ltd

All rights reserved. No part of this publication may be reproduced, stored
in a retrieval system, or transmitted, in any form or by any means, electronic,
mechanical, photocopying, recording, or otherwise, without written permission.

Commissioning Editor: *Masoud Yazdani*
Book and Cover Design: *Joshua Beadon*
Copy Editor: *Wendi Momen*

A catalogue record for this book is available from the British Library

ISBN 1-84150-032-1

Printed and bound in Great Britain by Cromwell Press, Wiltshire

contents

The world is changing and the role of the designer is changing with it. As consumers in a twenty-first century western society we have little choice but to collude with its information-driven materialism. As academics we (the editors) research, discuss and disseminate ideas about the ongoing place of design in such a world and, in doing so, have discovered a paucity of books dealing with the subject. As educators, however, it is not enough to merely hover at the fringe of the world of design, we should be at its heart and with *Becoming Designers* we aim to contribute to a timely, and at times provocative, debate.

This work therefore, seeks to offer a context within which to understand the educational needs and aspirations of today's designer. It considers crucial issues of new technology, gender, ethics, globalisation and internationalism as well as more focused topics related to the teaching of design practice and theory and to the appropriateness of current methodologies for doing so. To this end our contributors are an eclectic assembly variously combining the roles of designer, teacher, researcher, writer, sociologist, philosopher and public speaker. They have extensive experience of, and varied perspectives on, the world of design and, most importantly, all hold strong convictions. We are delighted that, despite their hectic schedules, they have proved united in their willingness to find the time to write these chapters.

The arguments presented, as one would expect, are as diverse as the authors and the opinions expressed are not necessarily shared by either the editors or by other contributors - indeed the grounds for heated arguments lie within these pages (we hope). The styles of presentation also vary and by limiting our attempts to unify them we have sought to preserve the individuality of each writer's voice.

Currently a mood of reflection about the role of the designer has settled upon the design world. The influential manifesto First things first published by Ken Garland and signatories in 1964 was revisited last year and has resulted in the publication of First things first 2000. Uppermost in the minds of the supporters of this revised manifesto are the social responsibilities put upon them as responsible designers. Clearly this signals a profession in a state of introspective flux as argument and counter-argument ring out around design studios (and public houses).

Issues raised in this book will be of interest to practitioners, academics and students alike and hopefully comment from all these quarters will fuel fresh writing. Indeed at a time when names such as Brody, Dyson and Lambie-Nairn are common currency beyond the world of design and governments extol the value to the economy of design, the book might engage a wider audience.

ud2k – designing the design student

Stuart Mealing

Stuart Mealing is a reader in 'Computers and Drawing' at the Exeter School of Art & Design (University of Plymouth), a founder member of their Centre for Visual Computing and teaches in the graphic design department. Trained initially in Fine Art, he exhibited widely and taught in art colleges for many years whilst maintaining an interest in the development of computing and artificial intelligence. He later took a post-graduate degree in Computing in Design and since then has been an Honorary Research Fellow in Computer Science at Exeter University, a founding co-editor of Digital Creativity, has published four other books and his papers have appeared in a range of journals.

With genetic engineering imminent it is tempting to prepare a recipe for the ideal design student. To define the sequences of nucleotide bases in the chromosomal DNA and the conditions of maturation that will, in about 18 years, produce ud2k – the perfect undergraduate designer for the new millennium. A Frankenstein wunderkind built to conceive, create, devise, discover, draft, draw, fabricate, figure, formulate, hatch, invent, mastermind, meditate, model, originate, plot, scheme, style and weave. In short, to design.

This chapter will consider what might be the desirable manifestations of these imaginary biological tinkerings as evidenced by the skills and traits of the monster itself, i.e. what makes a good design student. These qualities will also be considered in the context of tendencies within the university system (in the UK) that is invested with the task of converting this raw material into worthwhile practitioners. Is 'BA (Design)' the ultimate hallmark of a good new designer or might the academisation of design, in order that it can be 'read' as a legitimate subject alongside Law and Classics, have deflected the discipline's natural apprentices?

Any wish-list of key attributes is to be modified, not only in response to the changing needs of design in the real world, but also to the educational structure within which training takes place. It is implicit in the process of selecting students for design courses that there are qualities and standards that are sought by receiving institutions, though these are more likely to be tacitly understood than precisely defined. I suspect that staff conducting interviews across the country would reach a high level of agreement over which applicants are the best and which the worst but there perhaps would be less agreement on a prioritised list of the characteristics they believe aspiring designers should possess. Try placing in order of importance: drawing skills, intelligence, creativity, determination and literacy and state which, if any, are dispensable.

Creativity

> *Creativity knows no bounds. Its forms are legion, its sources obscure, its ways devious in the extreme, but its fruits are patent for all to see in every domain of human life.*[9]

It is hard to imagine a good designer who is not creative but perhaps in a design team there is room for people with a range of talents and their roles may not require the demonstration of 'classical' creativity. I have on my shelves a book with a title that appears, at first glance, from the smug viewpoint of one trained as an artist, to be a classic oxymoron – Creative Accounting. You can be creative within other terms of reference. To apply creativity effectively, however, it needs to be coupled with other things. In studies of leading artists and scientists Anne Roe[23] found that the only trait that stood out in common among individuals was a willingness to work hard and to work long hours. Whilst this is a trait that is likely to contribute to success in many fields, her observation threatens the uninformed impression of casual creativity offering an easy alternative to hard work. Thomas Edison is often quoted as saying that genius is 99% perspiration and 1% inspiration.

The characteristics of the creative act have been widely discussed and there is general agreement in the field that a mixture of rational and intuitive processes are involved and that the result displays originality. It is tempting to think of creativity as not being domain specific, to think that a creative free-thinker could have original ideas in any domain – (original AND useful of course, since to be original one merely has to be wrong when everyone else is right) – but originality is often a re-combination of elements into new patterns, which implies that the elements must be present and that therefore a basis of knowledge in a field is necessary to permit original thinking in that field.[22] It is necessary to study design in order to come up with original design solutions. Indeed most researchers suggest an incubation period for the creative act primed by thorough immersion in the subject area – 'saturate yourself through and through with your subject... and wait'.[21] Pasteur's famous dictum 'in the field of (scientific) observation chance favours those who are prepared' expresses a similar thought.

Interestingly, however, it is often the newcomer to a field who displays the greatest originality, as the more often an individual has solved problems with given ingredients the greater is the 'set' and the less the likelihood of attaining a further creative solution using them again. Our designer must apparently be both knowledgeable about the area and yet new to it. Hopefully for those with many years' experience, newness can be equated with seeing the familiar afresh.

Educating the creative

9 Research has consistently suggested that general education does not reward or nurture the creative, Rogers[24] for example saying that in education we tend to turn out conformists whose education is 'completed' rather than freely creative and original thinkers. Perhaps creative behaviour, typified by wild or silly ideas, humour and playfulness, is inconvenient in the orderly world of traditional classroom education. Conformity – 'sit still', 'be quiet' – is inimical to creativity.[19]

In a study asking social science teachers to rate the importance of cognition, memory, convergent behaviour, divergent thinking and evaluation in their subject,[26] convergent behaviour was consistently rated far higher than divergent thinking; nearly twenty times as highly in some areas. I suspect this still holds true across most subjects (and it is pointed out that convergent behaviour is more 'convenient' for the teacher). Other research from the same source showed that the learning procedures of highly creative children are quite different from those of children with high IQs but without high creative thinking abilities and that the highly intelligent children were described by their teachers as more desirable pupils, more intimately known, more ambitious and more hardworking or studious. Although these studies are now some years old, they still beg useful questions about the relative value placed on creativity in schools and on the level of reinforcement that creative behaviour is likely to receive.

Torrance[26] describes a student who displayed some of the most inventive, original and flexible behaviour found in testing several thousand children. His IQ (using the Stanford-Binet tests) was very high at 135 yet he was one of his school's most serious problems. He was not learning to read, had become a behaviour problem and frequently became so preoccupied with his thoughts that he didn't know what was going on in class. He faced a struggle between maintaining or sacrificing his creativity and the resulting problems of uncertain self-concepts, learning difficulties, delinquency and moments of schizophrenic-like withdrawal.

One of the first things that Rudolf Arnheim[2] established in his classic book *Visual Thinking* is that the educational system is based on the study of words and numbers.

> In kindergarten, to be sure, our youngsters learn by seeing and handling handsome shapes, and invent their own shapes on paper or in clay by thinking through perceiving. But with the first grade of elementary school the senses begin to lose educational status. More and more the arts are considered as a training in agreeable skills, as entertainment and mental release. As the ruling disciplines stress more rigorously the study of words and numbers, their kinship with the arts is increasingly obscured, and the arts are reduced to a desirable supplement; fewer and fewer hours of the week can be spared from the study of the subjects that, in everybody's opinion, truly matter. By the time the competition for college placement becomes acute, it is a rare high school that insists on reserving for the arts the time needed to make their practice at all fruitful. Rarer still is the institution at which a concern with the arts is consciously justified by the realisation that they contribute indispensably to the development of a reasoning and imaginative human being. ... The arts are neglected because they are based on perception, and perception is distend because it is not assumed to involve thought.

The applicant designer knocking at the door of a 'respectable' university may well, therefore, fail to match its broad notion of ideal entrant criteria. The creative adult was not usually an outstanding student at school[23] but satisfactory examination results are likely to be a pre-requisite of acceptance. If a course is to be filled from applicants who fit a standardised profile and are rich in examination certificates – certificates gained in a system which does not reward creativity – one can only conclude that many creative people are likely to be excluded. Experienced staff are able to make 'imaginative' selections for their annual intake but may have to fight for the right to do so in a culture where the applicants for most subjects apply on the basis of their expected examination grades alone. The knowledge of these criteria can also be expected to have deterred many potential applicants.

Intelligence

It has been observed that those with low intelligence are rarely creative and that the highly creative are usually highly intelligent but also that intelligence is no guarantee of creativity. Intelligence, it seems, is a complex set of inter-related aptitudes and abilities, some verging closely on the temperamental[3] and creativity too appears to lie as much in the temperamental-motivational field as in the cognitive.[6]

I'm sure all teachers feel that they can intuitively tell a clever student from a stupid one and amongst the qualities that amalgamate to make someone 'clever' (skilful, talented, quick to understand and learn, adroit, dextrous, ingenious, cunning) is intelligence – a key ingredient of successful, creative problem-solving. It can, however, clearly exist without the validation of examination attainment; indeed academic intelligence is of limited practical use without common sense and intuition in its application.

Although it might be convenient to be able to assess intelligence, IQ testing has become contentious and is subject to a range of criticisms about what it actually tests, now widely being considered to be biased towards mathematical and language skills and even to institutionalise racism. A useful part of the raging IQ debate has been the definition of categories of intelligence, Sternberg[25] suggesting: analytical, creative and practical, measured respectively by: traditional IQ tests, by problems such as devising an advertisement for a new type of bow tie and by response to real-life hypothetical situations that might arise at work. This offers a more useful perspective on applicants to a discipline in which, it could be argued, little is usefully tested by formal examinations.

Gender

Intelligence, whether measured or intuited, seems a necessary prerequisite for a designer but at the start of the 20th century women were still considered too weak-minded to be academically educated... It was believed that young women would fall prey to neurasthenia or some other nervous disease if they strained their heads with intellectual challenge.[20]

I do not propose to suggest that either sex makes a better designer; neither do I intend to enter the ongoing debate[28] about whether sexual differences are the result of nature or nurture. I do, however, think it is useful to air the different aptitudes, sensibilities and perspectives that men and women are variously credited with, not in any sense of competition but in recognition of their alternative values. The dolls versus guns argument can still be applied to career decisions and few would be surprised to learn that surveys have shown all bricklayers to be men but only 18% of librarians[15] or that boys are more likely to study engineering and girls to study languages.

Creativity, by its very nature, requires both sensitivity and independence. Torrance[26] says that 'in our culture, sensitivity is definitely a feminine virtue, while independence is a masculine value. Thus, we may expect the highly creative boy to appear more effeminate than his peers and the highly creative girl more masculine than hers'. Test results, for example, using the Terman-Miles masculinity/ femininity scale show college athletes with the highest masculinity score (+92) above engineers (+77) and above teachers (+45) with artists at 0 and homosexuals at -20.

Anne and Bill Moir[20] suggest that girls talk to their toys and boys deconstruct them; that girls tend towards verbal, co-operative games that exercise personal skills whilst boys engage in noisy, competitive games that test one another; that girls have a 20 minute attention span at a time when that of boys is five minutes; that in class girls pay attention and boys fidget; she is good with words and he is good with things. Sociable/competitive, quiet/noisy, compliant/argumentative, in agreement/ in disagreement. The Moirs are led to conclude that:

> *males and females are drawn by the biases of their brains to learn in different ways and to have different interests and enthusiasms, and any educational system that insists that boys and girls are the same, and must therefore be treated the same, is set to do damage.*

By the time higher education is entered upon, a potential designer has had 18 or more years in which sharp differences in gender trait are likely to have been smoothed by peer contact and social mores. Differences are less polarised but the underlying trends are still there. There are 13 mathematically gifted males for every one female;[18] women have larger colour vocabularies, better verbal memory and better performance on a test of finger dexterity;[14] men are more impulsive, impatient and more easily bored; women have better verbal skills but men have better spatial skills and hand-eye co-ordination (the old chestnuts about parking and catching) though women are shown to be better on spatial tests during the low oestrogen phase of menstrual cycle and better at fine manual skills in the high oestrogen phase.[20] One of the more interesting of the Moirs's observations is that women's brains cross reference more efficiently whilst men's focus better; a contrast between floodlight and spotlight.[20]

All these characteristics suggest differences in the way an individual will operate in a design environment. The choice of skills acquired and aptitude for them, the relationship with others in a design team, the problem solving methodologies employed, the briefs accepted (where choice exists), all are potentially influenced by gender traits. A design team (or design course) will have a greater range of skills and perspectives at its disposal if the aptitudes and traits of its members are spread across the gender-typical scale. This need not, however, be the same thing as equal numbers of both sexes if we note again that artists are shown to have a neutral score on a masculinity/femininity test and if we consider designers as being similar, in a meaningful way, to artists.

Art or science

Forty years ago in his Rede lecture C P Snow famously came up with the idea that art and science are two very different, implicitly irreconcilable cultures. F R Leavis and others have presented reasoned rebuttals of Snow's 'laughable melange of elementary error'[1] but the idea persists. Whether or not the two can be considered different cultures they are widely caricatured as being at opposite poles of an axis stretching from hard, rigorous and masculine at one end to soft, imprecise and feminine at the other. There are no prizes for guessing which pole represents which discipline – art is supposedly fun and easy, science is serious and difficult. Having spent blocks of time variously life drawing and coding in C++, I resist any argument that either, taken seriously, is either easy or uncreative or does not present an intellectual challenge.

But if one were to accept such a continuum, where along its length might design be intuitively placed? Somewhere between the two extremes, with illustration close to the fluffy, artistic end and industrial design closer to the tough, engineering end – and within illustration, the technical distanced from the editorial, within industrial design aerodynamics separated from styling? Design disciplines seem to embody elements associated with each of the two poles but rarely exclusively or in extremis. Whilst there are certainly differences between the aims and methodologies of art and science, some discussed elsewhere in this book, there is little difference in the nature of the creative processes displayed in, for instance, mathematics and art.[4]

Drawing

As well as traits, aptitudes and characteristics that derive variously from genes or developmental environment there are also learnt skills that may be considered important for designers to acquire. Drawing skills have long been considered the sine qua non of art and design. You learn to see the world through drawing; it is the foundation of visual literacy; it is the prime means of communicating visual ideas. At the time of the Renaissance one of the interpretations of the word drawing (disegno) was that of 'the creative idea made visible in the preliminary sketch,[16] a concept which embodies more than just the effectiveness of representation. Drawing is also widely understood to provide a rich way of exploring and coming to understand the world about us with marks on a surface describing not only visual experience but attitudes to them.

Hobson[12] reminds us, however, of the contents of most portfolios of design course applicants – of the stunning skills shown in drawing a green pepper from which we assume the applicant's capacity to be a designer – and suggests that the observational skills employed in exercises such as this (and in ubiquitous life drawing) are rarely employed elsewhere. Graphic designers, he says:

> should possess skills that enable them to make analytical, intellectual and conceptual judgements. Observation should be a prelude and an aid to deduction. ...By using drawings as our sole benchmark of creativity (as we have for centuries) we are denying access to our courses for a large number of perfectly capable problem-solvers and visual information communicators.

I am tempted to mount a defence of drawing skills from the apparently safe design quarter of illustration but even then I am aware of the non-visual components involved in 'solving' the problems in a given brief and of the mechanical options, e.g. photographic and digital, for providing visual output. I continue, however, to be impressed by the assistance gained through externalising a visual idea as a drawing, by the insight that goal-directed mark-making (a.k.a. drawing) gives into matters of space, light and texture for instance and by the intellectual gains from the rigour involved in the process. Also by the understanding that objective drawing gives of the relationship between eye, brain and reasoning. On each reading, however, I come to find Hobson's argument more persuasive.

He goes on to paraphrase Professor Richard Buchanan's reminder that design is not the art of expression but of forethought and cites Katherine McCoy (from the 1996 New Era, New Language conference) as saying that:

> Designers need a pluralistic and agile tool kit of strategies to apply to the universe of communications, messages and audiences. Appropriateness is the criterion.

I also find myself warming to his suggestion that linguistics should feature in more design programmes being, as it is, essential to visual communicators – manipulators of the visible manifestations of language.

Literacy

Perhaps the jury is now out on drawing but the ability to communicate with words has become a serious issue in recent years. It is increasingly considered that students from all disciplines graduate with too low a standard of literacy and that the reasonable expectation of employers – that someone with a degree be able to speak and write coherently and be able to observe standard linguistic conventions, such as those of spelling, grammar and punctuation – is no longer being met. An anecdotal reference by David Starkey in the *Sunday Times* quoted a 'long serving external examiner', after discussion of a scribbled and chaotic examination paper, as sighing, "I never thought to see the age of the illiterate first, but it's arrived". How, he asks, can young people of such talent and dedication have passed through 15 years of education and emerged, at best, half-literate?

I do not believe the assertion of successive governments that standards have not dropped and I know of no colleagues who do. Dumbing down is an inevitable consequence of encouraging rises in admissions which are unrelated to the talent pool and, with universities ranked amongst other things by their proportion of first-class degrees, it is understandable why this activity is familiar at many levels. Whilst there are, however, excellent students as there have always been, albeit in the company of significantly weaker ones, it is my purpose here to consider design applicants at the point at which they knock at the doors of a degree course. I shall not try to explain either how they came to be in the state in which they arrive or how the standards are set by which they are finally judged. In this context, therefore, it is necessary to consider what level of literacy constitutes a reasonable prerequisite for a design course and whether a design course should expect to take on the responsibility for remedying existing deficiencies.

The place of the dissertation on a degree course in design is argued elsewhere[11] but if the exercise is to be a meaningful part of a student's study then it deserves better than the uninformed, unstructured, ungrammatical, stream-of-(semi)-conscious-ness response it has been known to invite. It is also necessary to be able to communicate clearly to others – to clients, colleagues, technical services – and sometimes to write copy. But even more important is the need to be able to express ideas clearly to oneself as part of the internal feedback processes of problem-solving and, in addition, because natural language is a necessary step towards understanding abstract concepts. Being able to define a problem is a major part of solving it. Language is the foundation of thinking.

Computing

It is clear that all designers, both now and for many years, will necessarily have some level of involvement with digital practice. At one extreme web design will require deep immersion but even the illustrative watercolourist will need to recognise the constraints on hand-artwork which is to be reproduced via a digital press. The ubiquity of 'new' technology will render all designers conscious of the need for digital skills, although at some point in the future computing is likely to become sufficiently embedded for the emphasis to revert from mechanism to function. Many current design students are destined to play a vital and exciting role in shaping our experience of a digital future but Chapman, Fisher et al[7] find that:

> The experience of teaching students how to use computers for their design work suggests that three clear and distinct attitudes towards computers exist within every group of new first years – enthusiasm, fear or disdain. As they move through the three years of their course, it becomes clear that the enthusiastic students – usually small in number and already skilled with computers – rarely develop into good designers. They develop their computer skills, but find it hard to use these skills to produce inventive design work. We dubbed this group 'the nerds', and while this may seem unkind it can be noted that some computer enthusiasts take this label as a positive accolade.

Openness to the possibility (or probability) of using computers is therefore more important at the course entry stage than experience of using them, and experience of using them gained in other domains does not necessarily transfer usefully to art and design.

I do not, however, understand the concept of computer literacy any better than I would that of, say, electric motor literacy. There is no mystique to the technology. You need the skills of word-processing or image-manipulation or 3D-modelling and it just happens that the tasks can all be carried out using a box called a computer. You also need an appreciation of the appropriate uses of digital technology in the design field – just as you might need to know about the advantages and limitations of lithography, letterpress or gouache. But an even bigger red herring is that of 'keyboard skills'. You want a 'y', you hit the 'y' key – not a significant task unless you aim to become an accomplished typist.

Maturity

Maturity is an issue when selecting students for any high-level course as intellectual readiness is as important as satisfactory technique. Maturity tends to come with age, although old heads can be found on young shoulders (and vice versa) and older applicants are often welcomed for the extra experience and alternative perspectives they have acquired through rubbing shoulders with life for a little longer. Although the encouragement of 'lifelong learning' portends a new balance, the majority of students starting a degree course in 2000 are likely to be reaching the end of their teens.

I recall once being a teenager myself but am aware that the experiences, knowledge, hopes and aspirations of each new intake largely differ from mine at their age. Having insulated myself from the realities of modern teenagery through the strategy of not having had children I can struggle to understand the culture that informs them; (culture: the arts and other manifestations of human intellectual achievement regarded collectively; a refined understanding of this; intellectual development). It was ever thus. My classic films, revered books and key moments of history are not theirs. I know that almost a third live in one-parent families, that 42% have tried drugs by 16, that 14% of girls are unhappy about their legs and two thirds would like to lose weight though only one in eight is clinically overweight, that half want to own their own businesses and that 21% expect to be millionaires[27] but none of this opens up much common ground from which to share intellectual journeys. It is the discipline of design that will bind us together for three years.

These young adults are likely to have a very different attitude to the educational process in which they are embroiled to that of 20 years ago. Often explained as the product of a post-Thatcherite consumer society, it is not my intention here discuss the merits of the socio-political environment in which they grew up. It is important to acknowledge, however, that both their demands on a degree course and its demands on them have changed. Many seem strangely uninformed (Greenaway, Dickens and Hiroshima have all drawn blank looks recently) and this begs important questions about the extent to which the student must be fit for the course or the course fitted to the student.

Square pegs

Universities increasingly feel obliged to define the key skills that a student should possess on graduating – to define graduateness (sic). This obligation comes partly from government directive, partly from the perceived requirements of employers and partly from a culture of answerability. Bureaucracy appears to require that an illusion of order and control is imposed on the dangerously organic processes of educational growth and creative development. And so, administration having become the new guardian of academic probity, every course is decorated with labels deconstructing its purported learning outcomes, every detail is recorded in a tick-box. It is as if constantly weighing the pig makes it fatter.

> Like lifelong learning and the need for multi-skilled, flexible workers to increase our global competitiveness, key skills have all the necessary ingredients of first-rate educational slogans. They fully satisfy the motherhood-and-apple-pie test by advocating practices to which no one could possibly object, and they are so vague and nebulous that they can be made to include just about anything... The pursuit of such skills... is nothing more than a chimera hunt, a disastrous and costly exercise in futility.[13]

There is a conflict with the ethos of courses that have traditionally offered students the opportunity to discover their talents through a process of immersive

17

study; a conflict between mechanistic and quantitative approaches to art and design education. The prescriptive style is potentially at odds with the very variety of people on which a healthy society thrives; it militates against the extremist and the eccentric, the freak and the genius; it prefers grey to black and white – and creatives are rarely grey.

> Creative thought is innovative, exploratory, venturesome. Impatient of convention, it is attracted by the unknown and the undetermined. Risk and uncertainty stimulate it. Noncreative thought (the term is not derogatory) is cautious, methodical, conservative. It absorbs the new into the already known and expands the existing categories in preference to devising new ones.[17]

The creative individual is often seen as unconventional and associated with atypical characteristics. For example, anecdotal but informed sources suggest that there is a much higher incidence of dyslexia in art and design than in other university departments. Dyslexics are often visually gifted, their brains thought to be 'wired' differently so that their disposition is less verbal and more visual/spatial, which leads to a heightened intuitive sense of observation and 'clarity of vision'.[8] Typically cited dyslexic 'creatives' are Leonardo da Vinci, Winston Churchill, Susan Hampshire and Richard Branson (an entrepreneur who can't tell 'gross' from 'net'). Certain astrological signs have also been associated with creativity as has sinistrality (left-handedness) though, interestingly, ambidextrous children scored low on tests to measure verbal, reading and mathematical ability – widely judged to be measures of intelligence.[10] Whilst it is useful to note such attributes, it is unlikely that their known presence could play any part in the assessment of a student's creative potential.

Even the teaching environment is unlikely to be able to offer the best support to all creative talent. A design course typically (and understandably) is likely to present one communal work space for all and one timetable for all yet we know that different people work best in different conditions. Some need noise and some need silence, some need company and some solitude, some need very specific conditions. Dr Johnson needed a purring cat, orange peel and plenty of tea; Balzac needed to work at night with strong, black coffee; Freud chain smoked and Coleridge used opium; Zola required artificial light; Carlyle and Proust both sought soundproof rooms; Sciller needed the smell of decomposing apples wafting up from his desk drawer; Kipling had to have the blackest ink; Descartes could work only in bed but Bulton had to be fully and properly dressed.

The recipe

Napoleon wished for his generals to be lucky. That would also be a valuable property for a designer to possess but could be considered a secondary level attribute, accounted for by primary level attributes such as dedication and persistence which lead to immersion in the subject and conscientious practice, conditions under which luck is most likely to show itself. Our hypothetical genetic engineers should concern themselves with primary characteristics.

The designer of designers must create a product which displays an appropriate type of intelligence, is independently minded and is able to retain individuality in an academic world of grids and tick-boxes. Whilst some models should possess the personality factors which enable effective interaction in a team, others may be allowed to exist as self-sufficient lone players. The artefact should be available in both male and female options and must display maturity and reliability throughout the age range on offer.

It should be able both to express ideas visually and to express visual ideas clearly in natural language, though strength in one of these areas may be allowed to compensate for weakness in the other. Literacy and good drawing skills are likely indicators of these traits though either may, on occasion, be waived. Many other skills are coveted accessories that can be acquired later but, more important than their existence at the outset, is the preparedness to acquire them when needed and the mental flexibility to recognise that need. The top-of-the-range model will be zealous (inspired by intense enthusiasm), assiduous (hard-working and persevering), pertinacious (doggedly resolute) and with acuity (keenness of vision and thought) coming as standard. A random element in the genetic programming may also be desirable in order to throw up the occasional (but valuable) temperamental genius, infant savant or other maverick designer who will prove brilliant but awkward.

Of all the traits that could be prescribed for ud2k, however, my own priority would be for the creature to display just two, neither of which I have specifically mentioned until now. They are curiosity and rigour. Between them they will lead the student to enquire, to discover and to playfully extend the knowledge envelope. They will both make demands of the student and provide the means for satisfying them. They will lead towards novelty and will guarantee application. This heuristic pair alone provide the very cornerstone of the creative act.

19

References

1   Appleyard, Bryan. *Science vs Art*, The Sunday Times, Mar 1999

2   Arnheim, Rudolf. *Visual thinking*, Faber and Faber Ltd. 1970

3   Barron, F. *Creativity and psychological health*, Van Nostrand 1963

4   Boden, Margaret. *The creative mind*, Abacus 1990

5   Boyd Davis, Stephen. 'Educating the multimedia designer', in Dudley & Mealing (eds) *Becoming Designers*, Intellect Books 2000

6   Butcher, H. *Human intelligence – its nature and assessment*. Methuen & Co Ltd 1968

7   Chapman, G, Fisher, T et a. Creativity and the computer nerd: an exploration of attitudes, Digital Creativity, Vol 8, No 3/4 1997

8   Clifton, Dan (director), *Dyslexic genius*, Channel 4 TV programme, originally shown 25 July 1999

9   Cohen, John. *Creativity, technology and the arts*, in Reichardt, Jasia. *Cybernetics, art and ideas*, Studio Vista 1971

10 Crow, Tim, et al. 'Relative hand skill predicts academic ability: global deficits at the point of hemispheric indecision' *Neuropsychologia* 36 No 12 1998

11 Dudley, Esther. 'Intelligent shape sorting', in Dudley & Mealing (eds) *Becoming Designers*, Intellect Books 2000

12 Hobson, Jamie 'The end of the line', *Eye*, No 25 1997

13 Hyland, Terry. 'Skill scam'. *Guardian*, July 14th 1998

14 Kimura, D., 'Sex, sexual orientation and sex hormones influence human cognitive function' *Current opinion in neurobiology* 1996

15 *Labour force survey* Office for National Statistics, Dec 1997

16 Lambert, Susan. *Drawing, technique & purpose*, Trefoil Books Ltd., 1984

17 Langer, Suzanne. *Philosophy in a new key*, Harvard U. P., 1951

18 Lubinski, D, Benbow, C. P. *The study of mathematically precocious youth*, Ablex Publishing Corp. 1994

19 Mead, Margaret. *From the South Seas*, William Morrow 1939

20 Moir, Anne and Bill. *Why men don't iron*, Harper Collins 1998

21 Morgan, Lloyd, cited in McKeller, P. *Imagination and thinking*, Cohen & West 1957

22 Ray, Wilbert. *The experimental psychology of original thinking*, Macmillan 1967

23 Roe, A. 'The personality of artists', *Educational Psychology Measurement* Vol 6, 1946

24 Rogers, C.R. 'Towards a theory of creativity', *ETC: A review of general semantics*, Vol 11, 1954

25 Sternberg, Robert J. *Beyond IQ : a triarchic theory of human intelligence*, Cambridge U.P. 1985

26 Torrance, E. Paul. *Education and creative potential*, The University of Minnesota Press 1963

27 Unattributed, 'Going through a difficult phase', *The Sunday Times*, 16 May 1999

28 Walsh, Mary Roth (ed). *Women, men and gender – ongoing debates*, Yale University Press 1997

design for life: the lasting contribution of William Morris

John Astley

John Astley has for many years now regarded himself as a sociologist of culture. His regular focus of attention has been culture(s) of youth, communities, professions, music, the mass media and the arts, (including the 'lesser arts' !). He has talked on, written about and designed and delivered courses with regard to these. He is also very concerned about the inter-relations between theory, practice, experience, and theorizing, which, not surprisingly, requires him to examine the nature and role of character in regard to 'structuralizing' factors like culture. As briefly discussed in his essay, he sees culture as dynamic human creativity, both individually and collectively. These sets of processes, human 'work in progress', is very much about identity and experience, and vice versa, and can be seen as an antidote to the tendency for contemporary life to be stultifying. We live in a society dominated by inequality, privilege, irrational greed, moral authoritarianism and an anti-intellectualism that perverts the ways in which people might seek to lead fulfilling lives in peace and harmony.

Morris entered my life like an aesthetic 'Trojan Horse'; he was there having a significant influence on my development before I fully realized it. But, I have realized it now, in both senses, and it has raised my consciousness about design, about him, about myself, about creativity and been realized in my creative action.

It is commonplace to say that Morris means many different things to different people but he does. Anyone with such a diverse range of creative activities is bound to be interpreted in a variety of ways largely dependent on the values and motives of the interpreter. To say that what Morris has become for most people is a social construction is a sociological truism. But we do need to keep reminding ourselves of both the historical and cultural contexts of the interpretations of Morris and his creative output.

> *His largeness of vision is the key to it. Morris was his own emblem of wholeness. He wanted to integrate the city with the country, the present with the past, the public and the personal moralities. Most of all he was concerned with proper human occupation, whether going under the name of work or play. In the late twentieth century throughout the West this is our urgent problem. Technological advance has made ordinary skill and modest pride in work redundant. But redundancy of people brings the threat of disconnection from life.*[13]

Throughout his adult life Morris thought and talked about the juxtaposition of useful work and useless toil; how the former was found and lost and needed to be found again and how the latter must be fought against at a personal and a collective level. As you the reader will discover a good deal of what I want to say about Morris relates to this fundamental issue. For Morris art and creative work were absolutely crucial facets of the (re)humanization of people.

Pevsner makes the point that Morris wanted to re-contextualize art and restated Morris in that it 'has no longer any root', and on the question of democratic access to art, 'what business have we with art at all unless all can share it?'[23] According to Pevsner's interpretation, Morris defined art as 'the expression by man of his pleasure in labour' and that 'art' was a 'common culture' or, as Paul Willis would suggest, 'a grounded aesthetic'.[36] Pevsner argues that Morris was very clear that industrial capitalism, the prevailing system/forces/conditions of production would corrupt art, 'Art...will die out of civilization, if the system lasts. That in itself does for me carry with it the condemnation of the whole system.'[24] Pevsner has usually been seen as out of step in suggesting that Morris was looking backwards in his support of handicrafts production. But to his credit Pevsner did argue that Morris's 'decorative honesty' was more important in the modern movement than links with the past.

On the question of access Morris knew the inherent contradiction in the cost of his/The Firm's decorative products. To democratize them, to widen access, would inevitably lead to machine production. Morris was always concerned that mechanization would open the way for cheap(er) imitations. So the role of the worker/producer is critical. Now, as then, does it matter to the machine operative if they are producing Morris designs? Are they able to transcend their conditions and consequences of production in order to gain pleasure from their work? Is such consciousness any substitute for 'the work itself', is there intrinsic and/or extrinsic value in such labour? Because of Pevsner's perception of Morris as a 'backward' looking designer/producer, he argued that Morris was not a modernist. But as has been pointed out on countless occasions Morris did actually design for machine production, even if he then exercised very tight quality control over all processes from design to finished product. I want to return to these questions of means of production later on.

In this essay I want to consider the value of Morris's creative output, the 'end-products' of which are, of course, in the public domain. What I can say here about Morris the private person is limited. I am sure that he experienced many joys, disappointments and frustrations throughout his life; he was a man wedded to his senses, and was, by all accounts, quite emotional at times. So? He certainly had charismatic authority; people of all kinds looked to Morris to give a lead and this he always did, never shirking responsibility.

An example of this which comes to mind is Morris taking on the editorship of *Commonweal* (the newspaper of The Socialist League) from its inception in 1885 to 1890. He also wrote the regular news column in addition to longer articles. This was of course in addition to his design work for The Firm, his lectures, poetry, plays, prose story writing and so on.

What I see is that Morris used his personal self, with all the unique characteristics combined with the generalities of his time, class, gender and so on, to create a vast array of visible and lasting achievements and tangible artifacts. Certainly Morris was a practical man in the sense that he liked to do things (for) himself, he liked to make things rather than engage in endless abstract thinking. And while this is a familiar and over-simplified view of Morris's thinking skills, there is an element to him that reflects R.H.Tawney's famous aphorism: 'Life is a swallow, theory a snail.'

E.P. Thompson, like many interpreters of Morris, emphasized the life-long process that changed and shaped Morris's mind and life. Thompson rightly focused on the 'romantic to revolutionary' transformation. In sharing this view I would emphasize the remarkable journey that Morris made from individual artist at the centre of creative activity like Shelley; 'the artist turns into the legislator of the world'. To his lasting credit Morris increasingly realized the inadequacy of the 'romantic artist' conception of the action taking self and turned his attention more and more to collective actions.

I have said that Morris was a practical man, always designing and making things. It is appropriate to link this aspect of his character to his work as a socialist. 'Morris was not a man given to polite turns of phrase or to rhetoric. All his life it had been his business to make things. Whether tiles, or tapestry, or paper, no detail was too trivial to catch his attention. Now that he had decided that it was necessary to make a revolution, he set about the business in the same manner.' [27] Morris came to realize his own praxis: the free, universal, creative and self-creative activity through which a person (or social being) creates and changes his historical human world and himself. Morris came to understand his cultural praxis, his creative practice, in a way that was summed up by Zygmunt Bauman writing about his practice (which as a fellow sociologist, I would share): 'the practical success of sociology so understood can only be measured by the degree to which the opposition between consensus and truth is gradually reduced, and the problem of understanding as an activity distinct from communal life gradually disappears' (my emphasis).[2] I am also reminded here of Marcuse's claim that the real value of art lies in its capacity to challenge the monopoly of truth! Morris spent most of his adult life doing just that and in this brief essay I want to describe how he did it and the lasting value of his actions, including the enormous influence he had on the development of 'design' as a practice and education.

Before progressing further perhaps some working definitions of design, linked with reference to education, would be useful.

John Walker, in his book 'Design History and the History of Design' quotes Stephen Bayley: 'Design is what occurs when art meets industry, when people begin to make decisions about what mass-produced products should look like.'[29]

Walker emphasizes the Ruskinesque view that mass production increasingly separated craft from art and design.

> It was the gradual introduction of more intensive labour divisions, power-driven machinery, assembly lines, and growing automation which brought about the separation of craft and design, and which prompted the well-known debates about the fate of art and craft in the age of mechanical production and reproduction. [30]

In many obvious ways the emergence of Morris & Co. as designers was a contradiction in their aesthetic and socio-moral judgement of the high value of the anonymous medieval craft worker. One way Morris eluded this inherent dichotomy was to be a craftworker himself and not 'just' a designer, retailer and so on. Walter Gropius (of Bauhaus) was moved to observe that 'Ruskin and Morris strove to find a means of reuniting the world of art with the world of work.'[31]

Morris was always aware of whose needs were being met via the process of his designing. Is any designer really engaged with social production for the widest form of need rather than production for profit? Even contemporary examples like the clockwork radio? However, Ray Watkinson for one has stressed that Morris always sought to develop a relation between function, human life and action-taking. Morris, like many of his friends and associates, was very concerned about education. He was only too well aware of the failings of schooling in general and the specific inadequacy of art and technical education.

Colin Ward, one of the 20th century's wisest anarchists, sees Morris as a deschooler, fundamentally opposed to the oppressive and anti-humanist control system called education. Ward makes reference to 'News from Nowhere' (Morris's utopian socialist novel published in 1891), in which Morris has characterized a communist Britain without any formal schooling at all but where there is an abundance of life-long learning within the context of 'really useful education'. (And let us not forget that this was a Chartist slogan!) Morris as a Freethinker and secularist comes through strongly here.

I cannot resist quoting Ward, quoting Lethaby (an important figure in the Arts & Crafts movement and first professor of design at the RCA in 1900) '...those who believe in the condensed ignorance called Higher Education have succeeded with great difficulty in at last creating a dislike for that greatest of blessings, work.'[28] How things change!

Morris had a sound insight into the role of the media and had a few things to say about the growth and role of newspapers in his day:

> The quality of this joint product of paper-maker, compositor, and subeditor, confirms my a priori reasoning remarkably, for no adventure in this kind of wares has any chance of success if it has more than the merest suspicion of a flavour of literature or thoughtfulness...I will not say that the worse periodical is the better the chance it has of success, but that if it intends to succeed it must appeal to the habits that are as much akin to the reasonable aims of education as is the twiddling of a bit of string by a fidgety person.[15]

Morris often commented that the schooling received by the working classes was only good for the creation of discontent and that people are educated to become workmen or the employers of workmen or the hangers-on of the employers!

Not surprisingly, therefore, Morris and his associates focused their energies on the making of socialists via education and agitation:

> The work that lies before us at present is to make socialists, to cover the country with a network of associations...(who) have no temptation to waste their time in a thousand follies of party politics.[16]

There is a link here with Morris's opposition to the idea of state socialism; (one of the reasons why he was often dubbed an anarchist by those in favour of state socialism!) because what was important for Morris educationally was for people to have a vision of an alternative society to aid their thinking about becoming a socialist on the way to the achievement of a democratic socialist society. Attempts at creating such a society without the existence of people with clearly worked out ideas would be (is) doomed to distortion and exploitation by clever, manipulative rogues masquerading as the friends of democracy. This would eventually lead to failure and the triumph of reactionary forces.

By the late 1870s Morris was a well-respected expert in design. He served as an examiner for the South Kensington School Of Design from the late 70s and when the Royal Commission on Technical Education was set up in 1882, Morris was called to give evidence. In fact he gave 11 printed pages of evidence.

The spur for the Royal Commission was the increasing concern in government (and elsewhere) that the UK's industrial competitors were overtaking them and that the lack of good design and design education was a key factor (Along with the usual lack of sound scientific education). It was argued that there needed to be an inter-relation between art, design and manufacturing. The question was how could/should a set of art and design education institutions be established to meet this deficit.

One common focus for Morris was the effect of the division of labour on manufactured goods. He attacked the division of labour as both exploitative and short-sighted, as the resulting alienation of workers deprived them of any pleasure in their work or control over it. This process also led to a deterioration in the quality of the goods which was of course a key issue. 'Shoddy is King!' observed Morris

In his evidence Morris reiterated his view that designers should be familiar with both machine processes and materials in order to get the best from both. He also emphasized the '...commercial importance of originality and beauty. Originality was the linchpin of the Morris business; to a remarkable degree, the identity of the firm was a reflection of his own personality, thought and aspirations.'[6]

In his evidence Morris also advocated as much practical training in schools of art and design as was possible. Having the opportunity to see a design through all the processes to the finished product was crucial. He also argued that museums should be developed as places where everyone could see diversity of examples of good practice. Provincial museums, he suggested, should keep a representative range of local products and artifacts. It is always worth remembering that one of the tenets of the Arts and Crafts movement was to use, and be honest with, local materials.

Issues like this have been picked up by recent designers; for example in 1968 David Pye was moved to say '…economics alone will never justify their (the crafts) continuation. The crafts ought to provide the salt – and the pepper – to make the visible environment more palatable when nearly all of it will have been made by the workmanship of certainty. Let us have nothing to do with the idea that the crafts, regardless of what they make, are in some way superior to the workmanship of certainty, or a means of protest against it. That is paranoia. The crafts ought to be a complement to industry.'[25]

However, it has to be said that some people may see Pye's words as a palliative that would be 'the thin end of the wedge'.

Morris's great friend Burne-Jones said of him that 'All his life, he hated the copying of ancient work as unfair to the old and stupid for the present: only good for inspiration and hope.' According to Wilhide, Morris's great skill' was his ability to create something entirely new out of his enthusiasm for the past'.[32]

He used his, and others extensive knowledge of the past, and past art, as a lexicon, to be drawn upon and be inspired by. Over the fireplace in the Red House was the maxim, '*Ars longa, vita brevis*' life is short, art is long!

Morris's middle-class world was one of decorative confusion. The newly rich and self-conscious property owning middle class washopelessly uncertain which style to embrace. There was, understandably, a rapidly expanding market place for household goods. It was an eclectic nightmare, dominated by heavy, dark and cluttered interiors. In contrast, Morris sought quality and simplicity. For example his advocacy of plain white walls, where appropriate, had a profound impact at the time.

He was once moved to comment that 'I have never been in any rich man's home which would not have looked the better for having a bonfire made outside it of nine-tenths of all it held.'[33]

Morris was quite clear in these matters and wrote and spoke extensively on matters of decorative style. If, dear reader, you are unfamiliar with his advice you need to go to the original source and be inspired.

> *Any decoration is futile if it does not remind you of something beyond itself, craftsmanship involving not only the mastery of technique, but the evocation of the spiritual qualities of breadth, imagination and order.*[34]

During the writing of this essay I derived great pleasure from redecorating a room in my 1888 house with Pomegranate (or Fruit) wallpaper (1864) and a wild sage with coriander flat paint on some walls.

Morris is often characterized as someone close to nature. He certainly advocated a careful, reflective study of nature as part of design education. He did this himself and his prose, poetry, lectures and letters are full of descriptive references to nature in general and the countryside in particular. He was a great walker, often to the chagrin of his family and friends! His summers at Kelmscott and in the Cotswolds gave him great pleasure as well as endless sources for his designs. But he did say that drawing and design should be suggestive rather than imitative.

Gustav Holst, the musician, has just popped into my head – another great walker, who went on many rambles with his good friend Ralph Vaughan Williams. They went off collecting folk songs in addition to other countryside artifacts. Holst heard Morris give a lecture in London in 1896 and, after the latter's death in the same year, composed an elegy to Morris (a part of The Cotswold Symphony 1899/1900).

Holst was a young member of the Hammersmith Socialist Society (with his wife-to-be Isobel Harrison). He was involved in the choir and theatricals amongst other activities. Holst was drawn to the Society in part for its comradeship, which he felt was sadly missing when he moved to London from his home town of Cheltenham. These feelings in Holst were confirmed much later by Vaughan Williams: 'The tawdriness of London, its unfriendliness, the sordidness of both riches and poverty were overwhelming to an enthusiastic and sensitive youth; and to him the ideals of Morris, the insistence on beauty in every detail of human life and work, were a revelation. No wonder, then, that the poetic socialism of the Kelmscott Club became a natural medium of his aspirations; to Morris and his followers 'comradeship' was no pose but an absolute necessity of life.'[11]

Morris was not naive or sentimental about nature or culture. He knew that the Enlightenment thinkers had seen nature as rigid, as immutable, as controlling, and were dedicated to developing human culture as an expression of freedom and choice. Morris realized that a major problem emerges around the 'need' to control the potentially chaotic development of culture(s); too much freedom would be bad of course! If culture does need organizing, even policing, who is to do it? Is this a key contradiction in life for the bourgeois? It is fair to add that Morris was moved to test out the capacity of bourgeois society to make the fraternity aspect of 'liberty, equality and fraternity' actually work, let alone see the other two accomplished. Indeed, a good deal of what Morris wrote in The Commonweal (the journal of The Socialist League and edited by Morris) is that if fraternity (or fellowship) is not a living ideology that has transcended the dominant liberal individualist hegemony nothing much is going to change.

> ...We are living in an epoch where there is combat between commercialism, or the system of reckless waste, and communism, or the system of neighbourly common sense.[18]

Morris had learnt from Ruskin and other social critics the extent to which the factory system, the historical-inevitable consequence of industrial capitalism ,had led to the alienation of human beings, the sense that our own abilities and aspirations as human beings are taken over by other entities.

'Let us grant, first, that the race of man must either labour or perish. Nature does not give us our livelihood gratis; we must win it by toil of some sort or degree.'[20] This comes from Morris's lecture 'Useful Work versus Useless Toil', and, as mentioned earlier, this sentiment sums up for me so much of his motives. In his outward expression of these values it also became his vocabulary of motives. Morris developed an understanding of cultural, of artistic sensibilities and creativity early in his life. He was happy to the champion of such values and to take action 'against a sea of troubles' that got in the way. However, as he came to realize his values he discovered that the very nature of capitalist society stood in the way. In his first public lecture given on 'The Decorative (or Lesser) Arts' in 1877, he said: 'I do not want art for a few, any more than education for a few, or freedom for a few.' So he needed to take some action, to do something about it. Morris wanted to democratize art and society because he saw that the former could not be achieved in isolation. In this lecture Morris outlines the highs and lows of craft work. He extols the virtues of design by learnt/traditional skills, experience, and honesty to materials. He also celebrates the collaborative democratic processes of working that are lost to the industrial wage 'slave'. His response is to seek to triumph over this tendency by regaining control of the productive process. 'The artist came out of the handicraftsmen, and left them without hope of elevation, while he himself was left without the help of intelligent, industrious sympathy. Both have suffered, the artist no less than the workman.'[21] Raymond Williams reiterated this point about Morris and creative labour, that creativity ala art, and art ala creativity means... '...once you say that labour is creative, (it) cannot be confined to the notion of some specialized artistic kind of production.'[19] Or, to paraphrase Eric Gill; 'the artist is not a special kind of person, every person is a special kind of artist!' Morris had understood that the triumph of industrial capitalism had artificially separated out the artist from the workman, the former abstracted to the point of mere style, the latter to increasing degradation as the hand of the machine. One representation of Morris's vision of a society where this dichotomy was healed for the benefit of all is contained in *'News from Nowhere'*.

Raymond Williams consistently emphasizes the meaning of work issues, he is concerned about the way meanings, understandings, were deposited in a culture over time and were therefore fundamental to people's sense of what life and roles entailed (the interplay of the personal and the public aspect of roles). Therefore if work(ing) was forcibly/undemocratically changed, this central understanding would be shattered and replaced with what?

At this point I need to briefly revisit the question about the role of culture. I would argue that cultural action can be a pro-active realisation of people's desires and hopes, raising issues around a voluntaristic process of change, that in Morris's time, and now, would often be seen as utopian. In the late 19th century, the real context of Morris' practical ideas about change, utopian movements were considered as impractical by Marx and his associates. Marx et al conceded that utopian socialists of the turn of the century, like Owen, Saint-Simon, Fourier and Shelley, were understandable because they were not in a position to see the significance of the process of industrial development that would, in a dialectical way, inevitably create the conditions for the rise of a class-conscious proletariat and the revolutionary transformation of society. The weakness of contemporary utopianism for Marx was the insistence by such socialists that voluntaristic action by individuals played any part in the process of change. One of the reasons why Morris has often been seen as an anarchist (like Proudhon say) and not a socialist is precisely because of the former's deep suspicion of any form of hierarchical politics as an inevitable manifestation of a stratified social order, elitist cultures and so on. But Morris, quite rightly in my view, held to his utopian vision throughout his life because utopianism criticizes the present, postulates a desired alternative which requires effort/labour, by hand and by brain, to bring it into being, and which is certainly not inevitable given the capacity of the forces of the status quo to resist reformulations of the future. This is a constant theme in Morris, as with other utopians, embracing ideas about 'the earthly paradise', 'arcadia' and so on.

I am reminded of my introduction to a paper I gave at the Morris centenary conference in 1996, on 'The Soul of Man under Socialism'. This is the title of an essay by Wilde and my paper sought to discuss the links between Wilde, Orwell and Morris, and their profound influence on my sense of self and my creative raison d'etre.

> It has long been my conviction that cultural creativity can be an antidote to alienation. The expending of human labour, by hand and by brain, is central to our sense of self and the development of identity. We quite literally recreate ourselves through this creative action, we choose the road of dialogue, questions are raised, contradictions are sharpened and brought into focus, and conservative/oppressive forces confronted in the quest for transformation.
>
> I say can be an antidote because there is plenty of evidence that a considerable amount of cultural production in the name of enlightenment is anything but enlightening or liberating. George Steiner has once again recently questioned our collective (and private 'bolt hole'??) assumptions with his observation that artistic excellence has less and less to do with progress and decency. He argued that great musical performances, art exhibitions, drama festivals, architecture and so on have not only co-existed with political madness, they have adorned and celebrated it. So, yes, cultural creativity can be/are resources for hope, but ala Raymond Williams we need to look carefully at both the vocabulary of motives behind this private and public action and the prevailing conditions of production...Morris, Wilde and Orwell...are linked through their belief in the value of cultural creativity as an antidote to alienation, and their visions of the future, including the "education of desire". They were all only too well aware of Mannheim's distinction between the ideologies, or fictions that run our lives so much, and the utopias or wish dreams that we have.[1]

This does of course raise key issues about the organization of practice to which I must return later but for now let me cite Lethaby: 'designing is not the abstract power exercised by a genius. It is simply the arranging how work shall be done!' How different from my contemporary world of media – adverts – commercially dominated 'art'! To quote T.J. Clark, chronicler of Modernism '...art, in our culture, finds itself more and more at the limits, on the verge of emptiness and silence.'[4]

Morris came to understand the politics of culture well before he gave that 1877 lecture but, in the last 20 years of his life in particular, he interwove, like one of his designs, the development of his art and his politics. Morris referred to himself 'as a Modern' and this has not been lost on others then, and since.

> Politics, I should say, is the form par excellence of the contingency that makes modernism what it is. This is why those who wish modernism had never happened

(*and not a few who think they are firmly on its side) resist to the death the idea that art, at many of its highest moments in the nineteenth and twentieth centuries, took the stuff of politics as its material and did not transmute it. I think of...Morris.*[5]

Clark also draws Morris into his account of the role of the 'exhorting classes' and suggest that a good deal of this middle class rhetoric has to do with guilt. There is also here the issue of 'the civilizing process' a la Norbert Elias the 20th century social theorist and Morris was only too well aware of these pressures. Morris spoke on the contradictions of being a wealthy man and argued that it would have been futile for him to be philanthropic with a carefully managed portion of his money. Instead he devoted his later adult life and wealth to the socialist movement and the quest to transform society. It is a familiar view that the inter-relation between thought and ideal are central to modernism and this was certainly true of Morris.

A regular theme in debates about modern life has been to do with material culture, the objects that are produced (and the processes of producing them) in relation to our needs and wants/desires.[35] Designers/manufacturers and so on depend for their livelihoods on 'our' endless desire to consume goods/objects, which add to the stock of material culture. The value we place upon such goods is largely relative to the particular contexts of our immediate needs and our cultural contexts: who we are, our group membership, our values and so on. But it is also related to dominant ideologies, those pervasive sets of ideas that in an aggressive, or more relaxed and subtle way, persuade us of the appropriateness of (conspicuous) consumption, the quest for objects of desire, reaching fetish proportions much of the time. Marcuse, in his book '*One Dimensional Man*'[14], reflected, like Morris, on the stultifying nature of a commercial nexus. So to both paraphrase and take liberties with Le Corbusier on his definition of design, 'ideas made visible' is pretty open!

One of the key issues for Morris, as for us in the 20th century, was the extent to which the specifics of art and design have overlapped. Indeed what 'we' have done is to take art and turn it into material culture with increasing enthusiasm. Walter Benjamin's ideas on 'the work of art in the age of mechanical reproduction' are relevant here, and have focused attention on the 'popularizing' of art objects. There are many examples of designer objects taking on the aura of art: look at expensive adverts say (entering into debates about aesthetics of course, any Dada-ists out there?). It is more commonly the opposite that is true, i.e. more and more art has been transformed into material culture. More of us have gained access to these 'art objects' via manufacturing and therefore the nature of these objects has changed because of a wider range of meanings. This 'democratizing process' does not prevent art from remaining nonreproducible and valuable in this traditional way but it does and has greatly increased the overlaps between the motivations of designers and artists and also affected the meanings placed upon these objects by us as consumers, alongside whatever aesthetic posture we may strike.

Morris was engaged with thinking about how to transform the conditions of production in the 'decorative arts' to raise quality and increase access. He predated Benjamin (and others) in this concern.

> One of the foremost tasks of art has always been the creation of a demand which could be fully satisfied only later. The history of every art form shows critical epochs in which a certain art form aspires to effects which could be fully obtained only with a changed technical standard, that is to say, in a new art form.[3]

Fiona MacCarthy touched on Morris's constant drive for perfection, the quest that drove him on: 'I mean that I can never be contented with getting anything short of the best, and that I should always go on trying to improve our goods in all ways, and should consider anything that was only tolerable as a ladder to mount up to the next stage – that is, in fact, my life.'[12]

When Morris says 'have nothing in your houses that you do not know to be useful…or believe to be beautiful',[17] he means it! Unlike my contemporary environment dominated by the norm of commercial and monetary interest masquerading as aesthetic criteria and judgement. He is not being cautious or holding back from asserting his beliefs; he is a proselytizer for the development and deployment of the resources for hope.

33   I need now to turn my attention more specifically to 'The Firm'. I have already said something of Morris's character and his goals in life, his values and approaches to art and design. The establishment of 'The Firm' in 1861 enabled Morris and his friends to put their values into practice and, for example, to engage in the collaborative working model that they espoused.

> Having among their number men of varied qualifications, they will be able to undertake any species of decoration, mural or otherwise, from pictures, properly so-called, down to the consideration of the smallest work susceptible of art beauty.
> (From a Firm publicity circular of 1861)

Good technique and mastery of material was fundamental to Morris: 'As he believed that you could not design anything without understanding intimately how it was to be made, he taught himself one process after another.'[26]

When embracing a medium, technique or material new to him, he would spend time researching traditional products to learn how it was done. Hence his many visits to museums and the like. He moved painstakingly through weaving to embroidery to carpet-making and to dyeing; even, in this last instance, spending weeks mastering the making of the dyes themselves. If what he wanted did not exist he would make it himself or work with others to do so. A famous example of this was his creation of a whole new set of type faces for the Kelmscott Press. This sound basis in technique served Morris well and he went on to teach many other people, including family and friends.

So having established 'The Firm', Morris and his associates set to work. 'The ambition of Morris and his colleagues to set new standards in the decorative arts drew added strength from their realization of how well placed they were to carry out Ruskin's injunction to create the market rather than merely supply it; making products "educational instruments that would be more influential for all kinds of good than many lecturers on art, or many treatise writers on morality".'[7]

It is quite clear that Morris only 'went back' in time in order to go forward in design and production and in order to overcome the inadequacy of contemporary products. He was prepared to invest time and effort into getting the basic principles sorted out before he took any project forward.

> *Mere originality was not enough, as Morris himself stated "however original a man may be, he cannot afford to disregard the works of art that have been produced in times past when design was flourishing." Thus his textile designs, which at first were naturalistic and freeflowing, underwent a radical change in 1876 as a result of his discovery of medieval woven textiles at the South Kensington Museum...*[9]

'The Firm' became very successful and Morris was particularly identified with these achievements. Their collective output was considerable and Morris was constantly creating. For example in the decade from 1875 Morris made 21 designs for wallpaper, 32 for printed fabrics, 23 for woven fabrics, together with 24 machine-made carpets; plus tapestries, embroideries and all his other activities![8] (For those interested in more detail, Harvey and Press's book is extensive on the development of 'The Firm', in addition to providing a valuable overview of Morris's life.)

Once 'The Firm' was well established Morris also 'returned' to his poetry, languages and translating. It is worth remembering that Morris was such a renowned poet that when Tennyson died he was offered, and declined, the poet laureate. Throughout the growth years of 'The Firm' Morris stood by his principles and reiterated these key themes for a wider audience via his many lectures on art and design. This, for example from his lecture 'The Aim of Art' in 1887:

> Therefore the Aim of Art is to increase the happiness of men, by giving them beauty
> and interest of incident to amuse their leisure, and prevent them wearying even in
> rest, and by giving them hope and bodily pleasure in their work; or shortly, to make
> man's work happy and his rest fruitful. Consequently genuine art is an unmixed
> blessing to the race of man.[10]

And clearly one of the reasons why Morris championed the decorative or 'lesser
arts' was because far more ordinary working people were engaged in producing
fabrics, pottery, glassware, furniture, clothing, metalwork and so on than in
'fine' or 'professional' art of any kind.

In this respect Morris was constantly restating the golden rule of ethics, namely,
do unto others, as you would want done to you! A clear aspect of Morris's design
for life was to consider, speculate about and work out what was needed to
transform peoples lives via a revolutionizing of society, of social relations. His
critique of conventional politics also embraces the inadequacy of 'labourism' in
the UK: the trade union consciousness of limited demands of more pay and
better conditions within capitalism.

As I have mentioned before, Morris's fullest account of the processes contained
in this transformation to a communist society is in 'News from Nowhere', which
should be read by anyone who even vaguely suspects that all is not well and that
something else might be imagined and worked for. As I have already indicated,
Morris wrote and spoke about socialism a good deal and it is worth briefly
quoting him on this specific issue:

> ...what I mean by Socialism is a condition of society in which there should neither
> be rich nor poor, neither master nor master's man, neither idle nor overworked,
> neither brain-sick workers, not heart-sick hand workers, in a word, in which all
> men would be living in equality of condition, and would manage their affairs
> unwastefully, and with the full consciousness that harm to one would mean harm
> to all – the realization at last of the meaning of the word COMMONWEALTH.[22]

When I take stock of Morris' influence, it is, inevitably, essentially, with Morris
the complete man; the all-rounder, the holistic social-being; where certain key
values and principles formed the structure for his life and work. I have also felt
like this throughout my adult life. As a professional sociologist I occupy this role
full-time, I do not take on this self only at certain prescribed times during the day.
My co-existence as an educator is the same: I am always at it, seeking
opportunities to develop awareness and understanding amongst my fellow
beings, trying to raise consciousness and create opportunities for learning to

take place. This may sound horribly 'right-on' and pompous, but it has real intrinsic value for me; these creative, inter-active, collaborative and essentially social actions are life. There can be virtue in practice.

We gaze upon the artifacts and the processes, we contemplate the scheme and shape of things to come, our life and loves, our work in progress.

We engage texture and colour (once a Fauvist always a …), we would rather spend an evening in the deep red resonances of Dionysus than in the thin atmosphere of Apollo's company! We are prepared to stand by a commitment to authenticity, try to be honest to materials and methods, in preference to the endlessly shifting surface life of simulation.

There is pleasure to be derived from this focus on the value of human labour that should lead to the good, the virtuous society.

Morris has been dead for over one hundred years but his legacy lives on; anyone who takes life seriously, who is concerned with the opportunity for creativity and happiness for all, has a great example to follow. Morris's values, principles and approach to work in general and to a life as artist/designer and educator in particular, still stand as a model for us all. We should take up his invitation to focus on the issues that confront us today.

Morris has certainly repaid my investment of time and effort into his vision, his design for life. This essay is about what I have taken from him and why I value it. I also hope to demonstrate how I seek to repay my debt to him, in the full knowledge that without some commitment to reciprocity in human relations we really are lost, or to give Morris the last word, 'Fellowship is life'.

Bibliography

1   Astley, John. *The Soul of Man Under Socialism: Orwell, Wilde and Morris*, Unpublished centenary conference paper 1996

2   Bauman, Zygmunt. *Hermeneutics and Social Science*, Hutchinson 1978

3   Benjamin, Walter. *The Work of Art in the Age of Mechanical Reproduction.*, in Illuminations (ed. Hannah Arendt) Fontana 1973 p239

4   Clark, T.J. *Farewell to an Idea. Episodes from a History of Modernism*, Yale Univ. Press 1999, p.407

5   ibid. p.21

6   Harvey, Charles & Press, Jon. *Art, Enterprise and Ethics. The Life and Works of William Morris*, Frank Cass 1996, p.182

7   Harvey, Charles and Press, Jon. *William Morris. Design and Enterprise in Victorian Britain*, Manchester Univ. Press 1991, p.41

8   ibid. p.95

9   ibid. p.111

10   ibid. p.228

11   Heywood, Andrew. in *The Journal of the William Morris Society*. Vol xi no.4 Spring 1996, p.43/4

12   MacCarthy, Fiona. *A History of British Design 1830-1970*, George Allen & Unwin 1979, p.24

13   MacCarthy, Fiona. *William Morris. A Life for Our Time*, Faber & Faber 1994 p.vii

14   Marcuse, Herbert. *One Dimensional Man*, Sphere 1968

15   Morris, William *The Commonweal* 30.6.1888 (quoted in *The Journal of the William Morris Society* vol xi, no 1 autumn 1994, p.5

16   ibid. p.5

17   Morris, William. *Hopes and Fear for Art. Five Lectures*, 1921 edtn. (First pub.1882) Longmans, Green & Co.

18   Morris, William. lecture 1895 (quoted by Thompson in ICA Exhibition publication 1984), p.113

19   Morris, William. (in ICA Exhibition publication 1984)

20   Morris, William. *Useful Work versus Useless Toil* 1884, in Morton, A.L. 'Political Writings of William Morris' Lawrence and Wishart 1984

21   Morris, William, quoted in Briggs, As a *William Morris. Selected writings and designs* Penguin 1962, p. 89

22   Morris, William, quoted in: Morton, A. L. *Political Writings of William Morris*, Lawrence and Wishart 1984

23   Pevsner, Nikolaus. *Pioneers of Modern Design*, Penguin 1960, p.22

24   ibid. p.23

25   Pye, David. in Harris, Jennifer, *William Morris Revisited. Questioning the Legacy* (exhibition publication), Whitworth Gallery 1996, p.48

26   Shankland, Graeme, quoted in Briggs, Asa *William Morris. Selected writings and designs* Penguin 1962, p.176

27   Thompson, Edward P. *William Morris. Romantic to Revolutionary*, Lawrence & Wishart 1955

28   Ward, Colin. *Morris as Anarchist Educator.*, in William Morris Today (ICA Exhibition publication) 1984, p.128

29   Walker, John A. *Design History and the History of Design*, Pluto 1989, p.27/8

30   ibid. p.38/9

31   Watkinson, Ray. *William Morris as Designer*, Studio Vista 1967, p.7

32   Wilhide, Elizabeth, *William Morris. Decor and Design*, Pavilion 1991, p.38

33   ibid. p.43

34   ibid. p.64

35   Williams, Raymond. *Culture*, Fontana 1981

36   Willis, Paul. *Common Culture*, Open Univ. Press 1990

design praxis: towards a design context rooted in practice

Kevin McCullagh

Kevin McCullagh works for SP Forecasting, the research and strategy arm of the product design consultancy Seymour Powell. SP Forecasting offers services in management consultancy, social forecasting and design strategy. He graduated in Industrial Design from Newcastle Polytechnic. Kevin has held design and design management positions in four design and marketing consultancies. He has also spent several years lecturing and researching in higher education. He taught both theory and practice at undergraduate and postgraduate levels and conducted research into how designers use computers. As co-founder of Design Agenda, a think-tank on the relationship between design and society, he has organised and spoken at numerous conferences and written for various design journals.

Introduction

What happens if, when designing one's own web site with an intuitive and semi-automated design package, it seems as unremarkable as re-decorating a room is today? Or, what happens when we are just as likely to access online information via our hands-free mobile phone as a screen? These are but two questions that might vex a web-designer in a more reflective moment. They are two examples of issues that face designers of all disciplines. I raise them as an illustration of subjects that are unlikely to be resolved through past experience of the design profession. Answers are more likely to flow from a wider analysis of business, social and technological trends, wedded to a knowledge of design.

Design as a discipline is driven by social, economic and technological change or increased public awareness of design, globalisation or internet innovations. The key to understanding the consequences of any change is being able to distinguish between continuity, transience and real change. To make such distinctions requires a perspective that everyday design practice cannot provide. As outside forces are acting on the profession, an understanding of these forces is required.

Whether it be a design student grappling with their subject for the first time or a design manager writing a strategic plan, my point is the same – being able to understand design within the context the forces that act on it matters. What type of design do I refer to? All design disciplines with an aesthetic component, whether they are labelled graphic, new media, product, fashion or architectural, would benefit from a self-knowledge born out of reflective practice – or Praxis as I will refer to it.

Having been educated in industrial design, practised as a product and graphic designer, managed graphic and 3D designers, taught design practice and context and conducted research into how designers use computers, I now work in design strategy and social forecasting and I am as convinced as I ever have been on the need for designing in context. While I will make practical suggestions on how the current situation can be improved, I will finish by arguing that we will not be able to understand design effectively until we can place it within a general theory of design.

40

The importance of contextual studies

> *we can know more than we can tell* [12] Michael Polanyi

Contextual studies stands within a fine tradition of liberal education. The encouragement of critical awareness, the art of challenging and questioning received wisdom and the formulation and presentation of a coherent point of view are all critical intellectual tools for any 'knowledge worker'.

This tradition is especially welcome in design education as designers, as a whole, tend to depend on *tacit knowledge* derived from experience, experimentation and, to a large extent, an indifference to theory. This was identified as a problem early in the formation of the discipline of design history in 1981 by the design historian Tony Fry in his paper 'Design History: a debate':

> *Theoretical work, concretely and historically grounded, is not only of value but urgently needed in the study of design. It also means an expenditure of effort in the development of new theory, to address a changing design object. Further, I would defend this project as a site of resistance in the face of the strong anti-theory tradition within the general anti-intellectualism of British Art and design Education.*[6]

Tacit knowledge became a popular subject of study among management theorists in the 1990s. Their goal was to improve knowledge management – the way companies generate, communicate and exploit their intellectual assets. Designers and historians have much to learn from this work, particularly how to approach an understanding of how designers do what they do. Nonaka and Takeuchi, in the book *The Knowledge-Creating Company*, describe tacit knowledge as

> *... not easily visible and expressible. Tacit knowledge is highly personal and hard to formulise, making it difficult to communicate or to share with others. Subjective insights, intuitions, and hunches fall into this category of knowledge. Furthermore, tacit knowledge is deeply rooted in an individual's action and experience, as well as in the ideals, values, or emotions he or she embraces.*

> *Explicit knowledge can easily be 'processed' by a computer, transmitted electronically, or stored in databases. But the subjective and intuitive nature of tacit knowledge makes it difficult to process or transmit the acquired knowledge in any systematic or logical manner. For tacit knowledge to be communicated and shared within the organisation, it has to be converted into words and numbers that anyone can understand. It is precisely during the time this conversion takes place – from tacit to explicit, and... back again into tacit – that organisational knowledge is created.*[11]

It would be quite correct to point to any number of great designers who have created masterpieces without any recourse to theory. Designers tend to explore, understand and solve problems by experimenting with a variety of possible solutions, rather than by theorising about them.[4] However, if any problem can be framed in an appropriate context, the subsequent design process is likely to be more efficient and the resultant design better honed and more fitting. This is especially the case with new or complex problems. The importance of context becomes even more obvious when there is a strategic component to the project, as the problem has to be situated in relation to a network of inter-related factors.

Clarity in decision-making is harder than ever to achieve, as access to information is escalating. As designers experience a rapidly changing world, a knowledge framework to interpret and prioritise information has never been so important. Successful contextual studies teaching should help students locate such decisions in a wider perspective and consequently aid both their quality of judgement and its explanation to tutors, team members or clients.

One might also argue that a successful contextual education should feed students' creativity. If creativity is the *connection of previously unrelated ideas/concepts*, then a well-stocked mind with a knowledge framework on which to hang new ideas would seem a positive asset.

Speaking from experience of having conducted research at PhD level, another glaring need for a coherent intellectual framework arises in the debate around *'what is design research?'*.[18] A fundamental assumption of traditional academic research is that the area of study exists within a theoretical framework, and it is the role of the researcher to clarify the relationship between the proposition in question and the broader context of theory and previous research. Without such a framework the researcher is denied a language which enables movement from one observation to another and helps to make sense of the similarities and differences.

The arguments for contextual studies in teaching and research are reasonably well rehearsed but its relevance to design practitioners is less clear. The assumption tends to be made that when it comes to professionals, all the work has been done. Pressures leaves little time for reflection or questions of theory. However there are two clear areas that particularly benefit from designers remaining alive to non-practice issues: intuition and strategic planning.

Many experienced designers refer to the role of intuition in the design process.[15] By this they mean a subconscious 'knowing' of which direction to take in the early stages of the design process. This instinct about which ideas are most likely to bear fruit is usually put down to experience in the profession. In my observation, the designers with the most refined 'sixth sense' are the ones who are not only seasoned designers but also have a understanding of the factors and forces that are likely to make an impact later on in the project. It is their ability to bring a wider range of considerations to bear on a problem early in the project which manifests itself as intuition.

The three wise questions the design strategist Larry Keeley[7] asks designers, when approaching a strategic design project, are:

■ What matters to people?
■ What's next?
■ And how do you know?

Lazier members of the profession might reply that they intuitively know the answers to all of the above owing to the fact that they are professional designers and by definition in touch with what is happening and what people want. But most clients are no longer willing to pay for such bluster and now expect designers to be able to marshal evidence of research to support their proposals.

The problem with contextual studies

It might be thought difficult to construct any coherent case against a contextual studies education. But the common perception among designers is that it is largely boring and irrelevant. Too much history and critical studies presented to design students is often an attempt to apply social, cultural or art history theories to design. They rarely fit. Historians and critics tend to possess only a partial understanding of design, its processes and the forces that act upon it. The historian and critic Nigel Whiteley has pointed out that 'too many design historians make the mistake of seeing design practice as an execution of design theory'.[16] He argues that designers should be taught design history but that it should be a particular type of design history tuned to their needs. He argues that students require a type of design history that provides a clear series of perspectives in an intellectual and historical context. Such a history would be a means to an end rather than an end in itself, as it would be for design historians.

The central problem contextual studies faces is the mapping out of an appropriate territory. Victor Margolin, editor of Design Issues, has described the uncertainty over what the 'boundaries of investigation are for a design historian'.[8] After calling for more cultural anthropology, philosophy of technology, general systems theory and cultural studies, he concludes that we should move towards a field of investigation (rather than a discipline) called 'Design Studies' which does not 'close its boundaries to interventionists from elsewhere.'[9] I would guard against such an approach. It has led to an inability to make theory relevant and engaging to designers, which in turn reinforces many of their anti-theory prejudices.

Such moves would only widen the chasm between designers and theorists. Whilst I am certain that there are many useful insights the afore-mentioned fields could bring to design, they are not yet the key issue. Such a catholic approach might seem attractive in principle but in reality can only lead to more confusion. The more pressing questions are: 'who are the people who can identify these insights' and 'how are useful connections between these insights and design to be communicated?'. Only someone with a thorough understanding of design can make such judgements. When many designers have yet to be convinced of the relevance of their own profession's history, to introduce cultural anthropology is more of an affectation than it is a pragmatic initiative.

It is the lack of depth of understanding among design critics over what design actually involves that presents the most immediate problem. Margolin is openly uncomfortable with the idea that there can be '*a common understanding of what is intended by the word "design"* '.[10] He is right to make the point that ' *"design" does not signify a class of objects that can be pinned down like butterflies'.*

Design is constantly changing. However, it does not logically follow that design cannot be understood. All that is required is a practical understanding that embraces change. Rather than inviting in more non-design disciplines, why not first engage with actual designers and the problems they encounter. From this point of departure a coherent framework of knowledge could be developed that makes the insightful connections between design and other disciplines. An admirable goal for design historians would be to study designers' tacit knowledge, make it *explicit* and then suggest how that knowledge may be improved through exposure to knowledge from other disciplines.

Why we need a theory of design

> *There are few subject areas where less is known about itself than design*[13] Mike Press

Design students understandably complain that they feel as though they are lost at sea without a compass. The studio teaching tradition of 'sitting with Nellie' has many strengths but the transferral of tacit knowledge by example is not the most effective way of teaching all facets of design wisdom. Explicit design knowledge is best taught in a more structured and theoretical manner. While the mantra 'there are no rules' succinctly captures the current dearth of theory and is iconoclastic, it leaves students confused and the design profession ill-prepared to face change. If all we can do is explain the success or failure of design by example, how can we prepare for the future apart from wait until it happens? If a useful general theory of design existed, it would represent a huge leap forward in design education.

What design needs is a theory of change – '*a scheme of ideas which explain practice'*.[17] Such a scheme would provide a language which would enable us to move from one observation to another and make sense of the similarities and differences. We should not strive for neat definitions to set in stone. Such a theory should not only encompass change but also illuminate it.

What is wrong with existing theories of design? All have either been ignored by the vast majority of practitioners or have become discredited amongst critics. I will give a brief overview of the fortunes of the three most notable theories of design: Modernism, Post-modernism and Design Methodology.

Modernism

> Thomas Aquinas said that reason is the first principle of all human work. Now, when you have grasped that, you act accordingly. So, I would throw anything out that is not reasonable. I don't want to be interesting. I want to be good.[19]
>
> Mies van der Rohe

Modernism has been by far the most influential design theory of the 20th century. In the inter-war and post-war periods it was the dominant philosophy among designers of eastern and western Europe and North America. Its intoxicating mix of faith in technological and social progress, charismatic standard bearers, simple maxims and lofty ideals made it irresistible to a whole generation of designers. Its hold on the international scene began to loosen towards the end of the sixties owing to criticisms from various quarters. By the 1980s it was widely considered to have become discredited. For all its admirable goals, it was exposed for having dressed dogma, elitism and morality up in the clothes of rationalism. It suffered from being ahistorical and insensitive to the social and cultural components of design, often ignoring or failing to take account of the masses.

The modernist *style* made a comeback in the moralistic nineties. Stripped of its ideology it offered an aesthetic counterpoint to the perceived decadence of the eighties and a symbolic resonance with a more austere environmentally conscious decade. While many designers still admire some of the heroes and products of the modernist epoch, few adhere to any of the theory.

Post Modernism

> Less is more. — Mies van der Rohe   ...less is a bore — Robert Venturi

Post-modernism was more of a critic's than a designer's theory that became fashionable in the early 1980s. It essentially amounted to a loose genre of anti-modern criticism, rather than a coherent theory. Also the initial advocates tended to be French or German ex-Marxists, whose dense volumes would not have found themselves onto many designers' bookshelves. The first designers to seize upon the idea were architects. The Milan-based Memphis design group was among the first to experiment with post-modern product and furniture designs, exhibiting their first range in 1981 at the Milan furniture fair. In graphic design it was April Greiman and the Cranbrook Institute in the United States who led the way. But in the main it remained in the realm of the avant-garde.

By the time the term Post-modern filtered through to mainstream it was widely understood to be the name of a new and ironic 'bells and whistles' style.

The strengths of Post-modernist design critics tended to lie with observation and description, rather than explanation. Those designers who did dip into the literature might have enjoyed the wit and wry observations made against modernism – in retrospect, the celebration of diversity and complexity is of little use to designers. They have to impose some kind of order and draw conclusions for a living. Designers have to ask the right questions but, more importantly, come up with speculative conclusions. As the design historian and critic Adrian Forty has it, '*the whole question of judging quality in design, of discriminating between good and bad design, is essential to the entire activity of design*'.[5] Sensitive decision-making and the synthesis of complex, disparate and often conflicting information is at the heart of design.

The teaching staff at the University of Northumbria have made the observation that some of the brighter students have been inclined to engage with what could be loosely described as Post-modern theories taught in the later stages of the Historical and Critical Studies courses. However the tendency seems to be towards paralysis in decision-making rather than any clarification of the issues in hand. While this is only the experience of one course, anecdotal evidence from other designers who have 'dabbled' in such theories would suggest that few have found them to be of any practical use.

As a designer who has read more of this literature than most, I recognise that Post-modernism has contributed to a more sensitive appreciation of semantics, consumer taste and patterns of consumption. However, these insights have been gained at great expense. Its iconoclastic 'there are no rules' celebration of pluralism has helped legitimise a wider attack on all design and academic standards. Rather than amounting to a positive critique of modernism, in retrospect it has amounted to a retrograde step leaving designers more disorientated.

46

Design methodology

> the study of principles, practices and procedures of design in a rather broad and general sense. its central concern is with how designing both is and might be conducted.[2] Nigel Cross

A substantial body of work was carried out in the 1960s and 1970s on the subject of design methodology. Its major concern was attempting to resolve the apparent conflicts between rationality and intuition, logic and imagination, order and chance. This work was mainly carried out by academics, particularly in the fields of architecture, environmental design and planning,[3] with little contact with practising designers. The 'Design Methods' movement never gained credibility within the wider design community and by the end of the seventies was considered to have been largely discredited within academia. Indeed two of its major exponents, Alexander and Rittel, cited their own greater participation in design as the key reason for rejecting their earlier writing on design methodology.

Bruce Archer's main criticism of design methodology was that it was too logical and mathematical; it was, he said, 'A product of an alien mode of reasoning.' He considered

> that there exists a designerly way of thinking which is both different from scientific and scholarly ways of thinking and communicating, and as powerful as scientific and scholarly methods of enquiry when applied to its own kind of problems.[1]

While the design profession was largely unmoved by the activities of the Design Methods movement, the movement asked questions of design that had not been asked before. Despite its failings, important lessons can be learned from the experience. The study of design should not try to ape the methods of the sciences or the humanities but be based on the ways of thinking and acting that are 'designerly'. Design has both objective and subjective components and its inherently ill-defined problems require a fluid combination of rational and intuitive thinking.

Design theory – discredited

While there are national differences between emphasis on the teaching of theory in design education, few practising designers now see the relevance of what they know of design theory to what they practise. In Britain, at least, it is 'hip' to regard attempts to forge links between theory and practice as outdated and proved by history to be flawed.

47

The tacit nature of designers' knowledge, the indefinable nature of most design problems and the empirical problem-solving techniques employed by many designers do suggest that design practice is largely based on experience and experimentation rather than the application of a conscious theory. If design practice appears to exist successfully in a theoretical vacuum, who needs a theory of design? While previous theories of design have been generally agreed to be too naive, opaque or dogmatic, this does not prove the general irrelevance of theory to design. In the 20th century mankind has made considerable headway in areas such as linguistics, psychology and aesthetics; can designers really maintain that design is more complex, and thus outside the reach of theory, than these areas of human endeavour?

The reason that design remains bereft of theory is not a result of its inherent complexity, but because it is in the early stages of its historical development.

Design, as a distinct discipline, emerged out of a social division of labour following the Industrial Revolution. It has therefore always served the short-term interests of industrial commerce. With the exception of the much older profession of architecture, design has had little time to develop theoretical enlightenment. Owing to its relative immaturity as a discipline, it lacks the self-knowledge that other disciplines have developed through academic study over centuries, away from the economic pressures of the market. From a purely pragmatic point of view, design is perceived to have survived so far without the need for theory, therefore few designers see the need for it.

Towards Design Praxis

Anything that is not nature, is design (or designed)[14] Richard Seymour

Many shrug their shoulders and proclaim that design is too complicated to understand and ask why we would want to anyway. My founding assumption is that design can be understood and that a greater awareness of its processes is desirable for designers. This is not to underestimate the task. Critics are rightly dubious of one-line definitions and the numerous 'models' of the design process. Design is not a fixed process; each design discipline and designer within that discipline works differently, as do individual designers tackling each project differently. The design process is a highly dialectic, iterative, complex and – above all – human activity. Just like history, the design process rarely repeats itself. However this does not, I believe, negate a general theoretical understanding.

Design is about intention. In this respect we are all designers. In its broadest sense it can be said to be one of human beings' core competencies, one that distinguishes us from both machines and animals.[20] Neither chimpanzees nor super-computers possess our sense of purpose and intention, nor do they plan and set goals as we do. In essence, design is 'creative intentionality', the difference between the architect and the bee, and in many ways design is 'a measure of man'.

Any human activity which involves problem identification, reflection, experiments and proposals is a manifestation of the design process, whether it be arranging one's desk or designing a space station. While every human designs, a designer is someone who specialises in the subject. They make a living out of a range of disciplines ranging from engineering and software design to fashion and craft design. For our design is an activity which concerns itself, to some degree, with the visual aesthetic and is carried out by professional or student designers. It is my firm belief that any theory of design would have to start with a rich, human-centred understanding of the design process in general, as a process of conscious intervention in nature. It would also have to bring together a comprehensive economic history of the process of the division of labour which led to a distinct group of people specialising in particular areas of design and indeed it continues to provide the dynamic behind current shifts in the type of work designers do.

Universalism and specificity

Whilst on one level we should develop a universal or discipline-independent theory of design, such a general theory must also be mediated through discipline-specific understandings of design. We should not, however, get hung up on rigid disciplines and boundaries. They are always ad hoc static descriptions that attempt to categorise sections of the design community at a particular moment in time.

Currently the different design disciplines require specialist knowledge in some of the following fields:

■ Graphic design – communication, product differentiation, semiotics
■ Industrial design – product language/semantics, human-technology interface, economics and technologies of mass production, product differentiation
■ Craft design – intimate knowledge of materials, tools and processes
■ Interior design – manipulation of space, light, materials and finish, building technology, ergonomics
■ Fashion design – social aspiration, sexuality, gender, fabric technology

While it is becoming somewhat of a platitude to describe the dissolving boundaries between design disciplines, we should not underestimate the level of real economic, social and technological change that lies behind the rhetoric. The rapidly changing shape of work and technology means that the media most designers now work in is often digital and therefore easily transferable between disciplines. The digitisation of design is proving to be a melting pot for many design, and non-design, disciplines. As managers demand more flexibility, designers find themselves in many new situations.

Examples of areas of design activity where different traditional design disciplines are tending to work together and share skills, include:

■ Interaction design – industrial design, graphic design, anthropology, computer science and cognitive psychology
■ Information design – graphic design and cognitive psychology
■ Transport – industrial design, interior design, textile design, mechanical engineering design and Interaction design
■ Sportswear, sports equipment and luggage design – industrial design, fashion design, mechanical engineering design and materials science

It will be the detailed knowledge of specific design practice, knitted with a general understanding of design, which will be the key to making a design theory truly workable and useful. An admirable goal for the design profession would be the fusion of design theory and practice – Design Praxis. The motto should be: *practice informed by theory and theory informed by practice.* We should not counterpoise the two as independent elements. While they do take place independently, we should strive for their unity.

It is only through discourse between practitioners and theoreticians that real advances in design can be made. In the event of success, we would have a confident profession with a true self-knowledge and intellectual independence from other disciplines. Design would have finally come of age.

References

1 Archer, B. *Designing Design*, Design Research Society Conference Proceedings, 1980

2 Cross, N (ed). *Developments in Design Methodology*, p.vii

3 ibid. pix

4 Eastman, C.M. 'On the analysis of intuitive design processes', in G.T Moore (ed) *Emerging Methods in Environmental Design and Planning* MIT. Press, Cambridge, Mass 1970

5 Forty, A. *Debate: A Reply to Victor Margolin*, Design Issues, vol. 11, No.1, Spring 1995, p.16

6 Fry, T. *Design History: a Debate* Block (5), 1981, p.15

7 Keeley, L. 'Transforming: Reinventing Industries Through Strategic Design Planning', in: *The New Business of Design*, Allworth 1996

8 Margolin, V. 'Design History or Design Studies: Subject and methods', *Design Issues*, Vol.11, No.1, Spring 1995, p.5

9 ibid. p.15

10 Margolin V. 'A Reply to Adrian Forty', *Design Issues*, Vol.11, No.1, Spring 1995, p.19

11 Nonaka, I and Takeuchi, H. *The Knowledge-Creating Company: How Japanese Companies Create the Dynamics of Innovation*, Oxford 1995

12 Polanyi, M. *The Tacit Dimension*, Routledge & Kegan Paul 1966

13 Press, M. *Design of the Times* DRS conference, Staffordshire University 5 Oct 1994

14 Seymour, R. *Designing Dream Machines* Equinox, Channel 4, 12.10.95

15 Seymour, R. in *Design Week* Oct 1996

16 Whiteley, N. in his speech at the *Do Designers Need Design History?* Design Agenda debate, Business Design Centre, 14 July 1994

17   Williams, R. *Keywords: A Vocabulary of Culture and Society* Fontana 1983, p.316

18   For an excellent review of this debate see Frayling, C. *Research in Art and Design*, RCA Research Papers, Vol. 1, No.1 1993/4

19   Quoted in *The Conran Directory of Design*, S. Bayley, (ed), Octopus Conran, 1985

20   See Mike Cooley's elaboration of Karl Marx's discussion of the difference between an architect designing a building and a bee building an honey comb, in Cooley, M *aºrchitect or bee*, Slough 1981

intelligent shape sorting

Esther Dudley

Esther Dudley is a senior lecturer at the Exeter School of Arts & Design (University of Plymouth), co-ordinating design research in the graphic design department. She teaches all year groups across the specialist areas of design photography, illustration, typography and graphic communication. She has added to this role the responsibility for inviting guest lecturers who have particular interest for graphic design students but who also represent wider experiences and concerns from which students can benefit. She graduated from the School of Fine Arts and Music at the University of East Anglia with an honours degree in the History of Art, specialising in modern art and architecture. After some years spent teaching in international schools, she returned to her home in Cornwall, taught part-time at Falmouth College of Arts and took a postgraduate diploma in the History of Modern Art and Design. Currently, research interests include contributing to a survey of pre-mechanised memorial lettercutting in churchyards of North Cornwall and West Devon and a study of sheet music design and publication.

'I thought graphics would mean that I didn't have to write essays...'

It is a familiar scene. Each September brings its new crop of would-be graphic designers, diverse in their experiences and ambitions, brought together in the lecture theatre by an appointment on their induction calendar, indicating an introduction to design research. It is my task to explain the pattern that this study will take in the opening modules. In this first year of study design research will take place on Wednesdays, regardless of studio projects It will constitute a certain number of lectures and tutorials, concluding with a specified brief which represents the first phase of assessment. As the routine unfolds I sense that my new audience will have already made some judgements on this particular aspect of their course.

To some, design research will be no surprise. They will have read the student handbook or they will have remembered most of what they were told at their interview. They may have learned about it by that mysterious grapevine which springs into existence whenever students gather together.

I discern a cheerful acceptance, even a flicker of enthusiasm from some individuals, whilst sensing that a few take a different view entirely. They will have already designated Wednesdays as their opportunity to visit the dentist, or the accommodation office, or the television repair shop. After all, there are plenty of interesting things to do on Wednesdays. But all my audience know that nemesis must await them if they try to hide from the long arm of design research.

After explaining where design research fits into the scheme of graphic design, I proceed to say why it is important. I know that these words are going to be repeated many times, in an attempt to bring even the most estranged into the design research fold . These are the disaffected students who don't even have to utter the words of protest, so plainly are they written in their body language and on their faces: 'I don't read much....I haven't written anything much...ever... I thought graphics would mean I didn't have to write essays...' and so on.

'Graphic design will be the richer for graduates who are able to engage in criticism, analysis and debate' is the argument which I offer. This may slip by unnoticed in the opening address until I play my trump card: the dissertation, without which it will be impossible to achieve an honours degree.

This account has been written for the benefit of undergraduates. I firmly believe in the value of the concentrated research effort which culminates in the dissertation. I wanted the words that you are now reading to exist in published form, so that my spoken exhortations can end and I can rest from banging the drum.

Timetabling means that design research has to be allocated to a single day each week. Tutors have to be paid, lecture theatres have to be booked and courses have to be administered. The simpler all of this is, the better for everyone. Design research takes place away from the studio. It is no easy task to convince students that the subject is a natural, ever present function of graphic design. Studio tutors, I should say, are just as determined to draw the twin experiences of research and design together. Yet to the student it could seem that we operate with a paternalistic- and maternalistic-'we know what's good for you' approach, until they themselves see the point of it all. Frequently the assumption is made that design research is concerned with what happened in the past. This is a mistake as design reseach is very often concerned with the present. But in order to know what distinguishes the present from the past, and thus better understand our own time, we really need to know what has gone before. There is no reason why design research should not also be concerned with the future. Designers have always been interested in the future.

Back to the future of history. I can't think where the antipathy to the study of history on the part of designers originates but I am sure that the downgrading of the subject within the national curriculum has not helped. My perception of this is informed by talking to a history teacher at a successful comprehensive school. The history which is now taught in our schools nevertheless fosters some understanding of the contemporary world. Often, however, the new graphic design student has difficulty in conceding that design history could play a useful role in their education. Graphics, after all, should be about drawing and designing. The reality is that it is hard to think of a successful designer, graphic or otherwise, who has not been interested in history. History has vast treasure houses of ideas which wait to be recycled, transformed and turned upon their heads. Design has to be set within a social, industrial economic and political context. Then comes its aesthetic context. Christopher Crouch writes in his article 'Why Teach Design History?',[3] a compelling case for persevering along the historical route and suggests a concise definition of the designed object 'as the result of the interaction of function with ideology'. His contention can equally be applied to the graphic designed object and, indeed, when he refers to 'codified imagery' we are on very familiar ground.

> The relevance of a cultural literacy, the familiarity that a culture has with its processes and their relationship with other cultures, cannot be uderestimated. ...If aspects of a society's cultural life are valued and given prominence, an important arena is created within which social development can take place in an informed and reasoned atmosphere.

Philip Meggs, whose book A History of Graphic Design,[7] has helped so many undergraduates to research, describes his motivation for writing such a text.[8]

Teaching design history in the early 1970s, his goal was to construct the legacy of contemporary designers so that they could understand their own work, the vocabulary of design, and aid the profession in its struggle for professional status. He shares Crouch's belief in design's relationship to social development, stating that it is not merely decoration or style; it is a necessity for a healthy society.

Kevin McCullagh has written a paper stating a strong case for Contextual Studies. He writes from his position as a freelance industrial and graphic designer, and as a teacher of undergraduates and postgraduates, on the relationship between design practice and design context:[6]

> Contextual studies stands within a fine tradition of liberal education which encourages critical awareness, the art of challenging and questioning received wisdom, and the formulation and cogent presentation of a coherent point of view.

Departments of Contextual Studies can genuinely trace their history back to the monasteries of the Middle Ages, where the seven liberal arts which they taught included rhetoric – the art of using language to persuade and dialectic – the critical examination of arguments. Expertise in rhetoric and dialectic is essential to politicians, lawyers and academics. These arts are also useful to designers. What is much graphic design other than visual rhetoric? What is the interpretation of a client's brief other than an exercise in dialectic?

Students coming in to our graphic design degree course will be more familiar with the term 'contextual studies' than 'design research' as it is used on foundation and diploma courses. However, it would be wrong to allow the terms to be interchangeable as there is a clear distinction. Taught well, contextual studies fulfil the criteria described by McCullagh. The first year research programme which our students experience matches his description. But as their work progresses through the second year of study the term 'design research' becomes self evident. Increasingly, the study of context refers to the students's own practice as his or her awareness of place, role and responsibility develops. Design research allows the practitioner's own work to be the starting point for an expanded study, rather than placing the objective study of context, at a distance. If, in studying the context for their work, students choose to reject convention for the sake of experimentation, then so much the better. The choice should be an informed one. Experimentation has a rich contextual history.[11] Jonathan Barnbrook, whose inventive and sometimes controversial designs include the typefaces Exocet and Manson, states that his work refers to the tradition of type as an important learning reference.

> People should experiment, but they must know the craft first; otherwise there is no experimentation – there is nothing to work against. Plenty of students and

professionals think that they are doing experimental type, but they're not – they're just working in a fairly defined contemporary visual language. Experimentation comes first from a rebellion of philosophy, not just a rebellion of style.[1]

Wisdom is better than rubies

Ilustration historian Leo DeFreitas, who is a visiting lecturer to our course, told of a proverb for the digital age, which he found whilst surfing the net:

Data is not information, information is not knowledge, knowledge is not wisdom.[12]

The curious thing is that the OED definition of each of these words refers to the next in the series – data is defined as information, and so on. Therefore, in linguistic terms, the statement appears to make little sense. Yet in research it is crystal clear and serves as an indicator of what we expect students to achieve through engaging at a sufficient level with their chosen subject. We hope to see the transformation of data into information, the examination and critical analysis of which can lead to understanding and a specialised knowledge. This is the true value of the dissertation. Of course, we cannot guarantee that any student will possess wisdom on completing the course. Wisdom, by its very nature, cannot be imposed. Yet the ambition to acquire wisdom is of the utmost importance in the development of each one of us. Wisdom is attained by the experience of gaining knowledge and understanding, not only of one's subject, but also of oneself.

Receive my instruction, and not silver; and knowledge rather than gold. For wisdom is better than rubies; and all things that may be desired are not to be compared to it.[9]

This Old Testament injunction is as inspirational today as when it was uttered those millennia ago.

57

The dissertation became a formal requirement of art and design education in the wake of the Coldstream Report of 1960 which recommended that the traditional craft-based courses should be replaced by specialist arts subjects. This report was of immense importance in the history of design education. It marked the first official recognition that Art and Design were comparable, intellectually, with the conventional academic subjects – English, History, Geography and so forth. Graphic design was established as a major subject, though not all art colleges were recognised for the delivery of a range of subjects. Exeter College of Art, for instance, was at first only allocated a fine art course.[5] Nikolaus Pevsner, as a member of the committee which drafted the report, pressed for the implementation of an art education system in which everyone should have a course in liberal studies and Art History – and by implication Design History –

and Complementary Studies. The importance of this area of study is clear from the following statements in the Report:

> We see a prime objective of complementary studies as being to enable the student to understand relationships between his own activites and the culture within which he lives as it has evolved.

> Complementary studies should be an integral part of the student's art and design education, informing but not dictating to the creative aspects of his work.[10]

This was written at a time when the masculine personal pronouns were used without question. But the Coldstream Report has stood the test of time and we owe much to it.

The Diploma in Art and Design was elevated to the level of a degree course as the polytechnics, which were later given university status, took over the bulk of the provision of art education. The written component in courses was not inserted to exclude the less academically inclined student but to ensure that all students would be able to view their own disciplines in a critical way. The dissertation became a key component in a degree which was intended to have authentic academic credibility.

At the Making/Writing Conference which was held in Exeter in 1998, we discussed the differences and affinities of both activities. Our starting assumption was that neither making nor writing should be assumed to take intellectual precedence over the other. Instead, they should reflect characteristics of each other. The maker and the writer could both be described as originators, or creators, with the outcome of their efforts being dictated by external demands. Pavel Buchler's keynote address led us into the theme:

> To comprehend writing and making as modes, one must look not at the final product but at the potential contained in the original thought itself. There are undoubtedly perceptions and ideas which call for being articulated in writing, becoming texts, and others which demand being shaped by making to become objects or images. But in the main, it is likely that thoughts, perceptions or ideas will contain a range of such potentials simultaneously (including, most obviously the potential for nothing being done about them at all) and the heirarchy of the modes that may be deployed in realising a particular potential will be a matter of external priorities.[2]

In academic institutions priorities are usually imposed by those who shape the structure for learning. Paula J. Curran has described the structure and brief of the course she has devised entitled 'Designing with Self-Authored Text'[4] in which she challenges the historical role of designers as mediators rather than creators of text. There is an obviousness to the process of integrating writing and design that is often overlooked, though they share the simple stages of production: research, creative thought, planning, drafts and refinement. It seems the course allows every opportunity to the student to develop a solution to a verbal and visual communication problem and, at the same time, keep a notebook to record the process, a necessary tool in the task of self-criticism and self-evaluation. This is a model we could well consider adopting.

The dissertation is the outcome of a period of intense, self-driven research. This is its supreme value. It is a significant rite of intellectual passage: the authoring of a text which is to be validated by academic authority. Yet despite the recognition of its importance, pressures may be brought to bear on studio-based courses which could threaten the continuation of the dissertation as an essential element. In the climate of diminishing resources, departments are forced to consider reducing the time spent on teaching. In the event of a student failing a module, no extra teaching is available and a sub-standard piece might be accepted as a re-submission for the sake of moving the student onto a module at which he or she is likely to achieve greater success. Some students experience difficulty with the written element. It is easy to see how the lowering of expectations would undermine the important role the dissertation has for what is, after all, the majority of students.

A former designer for television who has devoted the latter part of his career to design education, recently recalled his time at the BBC. We were actually talking about dissertations. He recalled excellent designers who never got the best plays or shows to design because they were unable to express their ideas fluently, whether in conversation or writing. Directors and programme planners, whose lives are frenetic, have little time for mumbled or written gabble.

‘Literacy and the ability to express ideas to colleagues and clients,’ said my friend, ‘are part of the indispensable armoury of the designer.’

An inability to manipulate language is a great disadvantage for a graphic designer. Linguistic laissez-faire should not be condoned. Language is common property and to function it should be widely understood. Jargon, the language of coteries, is swiftly superseded by other jargon. Designers need to make words and images perform on comparable conceptual levels. Credibility for the designer is gained when this is achieved, yet undermined when there is poor control over the mechanics of language. The discipline that gaining such control inevitably requires should be encouraged and the skill of writing coherently mastered. The reality is that writing is as vital to the graphic designer as the making of dovetail joints is to the cabinet maker.

Learning how to use a university library is most important for the student graphic designer. Students are expected to engage with the literature of their subject. By researching and writing we can appreciate more readily the dedication of those authors who bring our subject to life, pushing forward debate and criticism. The discovery of alternative methodologies is essential if our viewpoints are to mature. In order to nourish the creative process, the fledgling designer needs to be aware of how texts and images have been related to each other, not only in the past but also in the present. Design journalism is alive with comment and debate that the student cannot afford to ignore. The activity of engaging with it on a regular basis is so important that it forms a basis for project work which is assessed in the first design research module that I teach. One expects that the practice, once established, continues throughout the degree course and beyond, into professional life. All professions, industries and trades rely on discussion and comment, as the diversity of this area of publishing shows.

Thomas Edison said, 'Genius is ninety-nine percent perspiration and one percent inspiration.' The perspiration/inspiration battle applies equally to the research and writing process as it does to the grand gesture of the finished designed piece. It is rewarding to observe, as students work on their projects, the development of their ideas and the self-criticism which inevitably arises. I tutor a very wide range of dissertation subjects, as a member of a graphic design department which offers typography, illustration and photography as specialisms. Last year's crop yielded, amongst many, Sign Language: A Study of British Road Signage by a typographer; Mailart by an illustrator; another typographer's investigation of the branding of Britain via the Dome; and a study of the relationship of photographer, subject and viewer with reference to the work of Hannah Starkey, by a design photographer. The current year displays a fascination for all things digital, as might be expected, with attempts being made to be expert in the area of web design and multi media programmes. Here students are acting upon the advice to envisage the route they wish their career to take and prepare for it through the dissertation research.

Any teacher should acknowledge that we learn as much as we teach. The satisfaction gained in tutoring dissertation students derives, in part, from the vicarious experience of research into a subject that one may not have been particularly familiar with before. Such subjects often have a contemporary story which unfolds as the dissertation proceeds. It can be a challenge to keep up with the latest twists and turns, gleaning information to pass on in tutorials, whenever the opportunity arises. We are still able to provide one-to-one tutorials throughout the dissertation module. This is an expensive teaching method and there is funding for just four tutorials. This concentrates the minds and efforts of tutor and student. My ex-television designer friend remarks on this form of teaching:

This is a tried and proven method which invariably produces results commensurate with the student's ability. Often, however, a previously indistinguished student blossoms under the one-to-one tutorial system. I fervently hope that this kind of teaching can be maintained in the future. It is the very life blood of design education.

Concerned that the dissertation may have assumed a disproportionate meaning for me because so many of my efforts are directed towards it, I asked the opinion of my colleague Katy McCleod. We agreed on the broad themes that I have touched upon, but with characteristic precision Katy added:

Writing an extended essay or thesis deepens a student's engagement with their practice. It serves to clarify their practice concerns.

The dissertation is a measure of students' depth of engagement with their own practices and the text . Confronting one's own demons is never a comfortable experience. But what a triumph it is to overcome them and produce work that has tested us on deeper levels and succeeded.

At times, in tutorials, as the student worries over the structure of the piece, I am reminded of the shape sorter toys that the Early Learning Centre convinced me to buy when my children were very young. Shape sorter toys would aid their hand and eye coordination. No doubt the parents of many of my students were convinced by the same argument. They would, I am sure, be proud of their offspring as they sort their present precious shapes into the structures of their own devising.

The dissertation is the moment of intelligent shape sorting.

References/notes

1. Barnbrook, Jonathan. 'Experimentation' in Heller, Steven and Pettit, Elinor. *Design Dialogues* Allworth Press, New York 1998

2. Buchler, Pavel. *Words Apart: the Question of Authority*, a paper for Making/Writing conference, Exeter, September 1998

3. Crouch, Christopher. 'Why Teach Design History?' in Thistlewood, David (ed.) *Issues in Design Education*, Longman 1990

4. Curran, Paula J. 'Designing with Self-Authored Text ' in Heller, Steven (ed.) *The Education of a Graphic Designer*, Allworth Press, New York 1998

5. In conversation with David Jeremiah, Head of School, Exeter School of Art & Design, University of Plymouth until 1994

6. McCullagh, Kevin. *Towards a Design Context Rooted in Design Practice*, a paper for Contextual Design, Design in Contexts, The European Academy of Design conference, Stockholm, April 1997

7   Meggs, Philip. *A History of Graphic Design*, 2nd ed. Van Nostrand Reinhold, New York 1992

8   Meggs, Philip. 'Graphic Design History' in Heller, Steven and Pettit, Elinor. *Design Dialogues*, Allworth Press, New York 1998

9.   Proverbs 8: 10,11.

10   Warren Piper, David (ed.). *Readings in Art and Design Education after the Coldstream Report*, Davis Poynter 1973

11   Poynor, Rick. *Design Without Boundaries*, Booth-Clibborn Editions 1998

12   Source unknown, yet not far removed from T.S. Eliot's chorus in *The Rock*, a pageant play, 1934:

Where is the wisdom that we have lost in knowledge?

Where is the knowledge that we have lost in information?

educating the multimedia designer

Stephen Boyd Davis

Stephen Boyd Davis has taught full-time in FE and HE, in independent art schools and university departments and has undertaken the validation and external examining of other courses. He is co-founder of the innovative masters' course in Interactive Media at Middlesex University. As a graduate of art school, he is particularly interested in identifying the strengths of that tradition and building on them.

Introduction

Interactive multimedia can be taught in a number of higher education environments, including both Art and Design and Computer Science, and each environment has its own traditions of educational practice. I hope to draw out the strengths and weaknesses of these different traditions and at the same time make suggestions about the nature of design which have an impact (or should do) on what we teach and how it is learned. By showing how the educational approach is inseparable from the underlying design philosophy, I aim to highlight some problems of design theory as well as questioning inherited educational practices.

A fundamental assumption in all that follows is that teaching and learning are not the same thing. Students on a course may learn far more (as well as less) than is explicitly taught. Factors other than the curriculum content will significantly influence the outcome. To begin, I will describe what seem to me the salient features of art school education, emphasising those aspects which are not simply curricular.

Nature of the art school approach

The art school, whether independent or as a department of a larger institution, offers a distinctive tradition which differs significantly from most other forms of higher education. This continues despite diminishing resources. Special characteristics include: individual experimentation, a close contact with materials and technologies, and an encouragement to take risks and to explore the limits of the subject. Typically students enjoy four years of study to bachelor's level which includes a wide-ranging diagnostic Foundation course. Their work consists largely of projects. Examinations of a traditional kind are rare. First-hand experience is valued above textual description. While many projects involve a brief set by staff, the responses are 'owned' by the students, who see them as part of their own personal development. High levels of motivation are common. Students learn important skills through undertaking project work and research, many skills which are never explicitly taught. This approach emphasises the experiential nature of design, acknowledging that designers are best able to innovate when they have an intimate understanding of their craft brought about by extensive practical experience[14] and that a high level of critical awareness of the potentialities of the media and tools available is essential to creative activity.[31] In addressing US educational policy, Shneiderman[34] has argued passionately for 'engagement', which he defines as interaction with people, and 'construction' – students as creators. Importantly, neither of these is a taught subject but a mode of learning and both have been fundamental to art and design education for decades. Indeed these ideas have a long history, going back at least to Dewey,[5] and some aspects of this tradition have been taken up elsewhere. For example,

64

there has been increasing interest in the portfolio as a representation of a student's accumulated achievements and many disciplines now use at least a proportion of student-led practical projects but it is still true to say that they are the norm for Art and Design and the exception for other forms of higher education.

I want to focus not on the strengths but on the weaknesses of Art and Design methods. Interactive Multimedia makes a particularly useful case study since it is a subject taught in two quite different ways depending on the educational tradition in which it is situated. Computer Science departments have over the years been giving increasing attention to the study of Human–Computer Interaction and, given that most computing is now by nature multimedia, this activity has a great deal in common with Interactive Multimedia as it is understood within Art and Design. These two different educational traditions – Science and Technology and Art and Design – have little common ground.

The challenge of multimedia design

Interactive Multimedia places some special demands on the designer. Designers must be able to give form to concept and content using an exceptionally wide range of disparate elements including graphics, music and sound, typography, text, animation and filmic imagery, all in an interactive context. The artefacts produced include fiction and non-fiction CDs, games, websites, various kinds of interactive television and prototypes for new kinds of interactive products, such as innovative telecommunications devices. Such artefacts dominate the European industry, omitting an element important in the United States: the design of interactive tools such as the kinds of software most of us use every day; European software (in this sense) is almost non-existent. Another regional difference is in the size of companies. US companies are often very large, while their European counterparts mainly comprise small and very small enterprises. Even though large organisations such as broadcasters and telecommunications companies are involved in interactive multimedia, much of this work is subcontracted to the very small companies. This emphasises the need for designers to be multi-skilled, flexible and good at interrelating with others.

Guesses about future uses of new technologies are generally wrong[20,21] and interactive multimedia is in a state of rapid change. Only five years ago one could have run a course in the subject without mentioning the World Wide Web! At the same time, many book publishers who attempted to move into CD-ROM publishing have had their fingers burned. At the time of writing there is an explosion of interest in interactive television. There is not only a convergence of various technologies but also of their inherited practices.[24,2] Many multimedia products still bear clearly the fingerprints of the particular trades which have produced them: of television, of book publishing or of database design. In education we need to turn this rag-bag of practices into an integrated subject: an approach which merely adds together modules in sound, image, text, narrative , etc. will not enable students to achieve this integrated view.[4] It will be a course in multiple media, not multimedia, and risk omitting the two single most important constituents of the subject: integration and interaction.

Problems of the art school tradition

There are a number of aspects of the art school tradition which seem to me counter-productive in the face of these challenges. I believe that they are equally unhelpful in relation to other design disciplines.

Monotechnic intake

Art schools are full of artists; at least, they are dominated by students who have done art at school and who, thanks to the restrictive tendencies of school timetabling, were encouraged to drop scientific and technological subjects. The single-discipline culture of the art school department leads to a number of problems, often exacerbated by departmental rivalries which even militate against collaboration between, say, painters and textile designers. Students' ability to understand and communicate with those from different disciplines is often poor. Their range of conceptual skills tends to be narrow so that, for example, they are weak at using any sort of objective or quantitative approach. In fact, such an approach will generally not even occur to them unprompted. And they are likely to have a rather narrow range of design methods at their command; for example, excluding most kinds of analysis and planning.

Anti-intellectualism

This monotechnic culture, this lack of exposure to other ways of thinking, in turn aggravates another difficulty. The very emphasis on practical experience in preference to second-hand knowledge, which is a strength of the art school, militates against effective use of written knowledge. It is as if *everything* must be discovered first hand in order to be valid. The majority of art students begrudge the theoretical component of their studies, regarding it as a distraction from what they are really there to do. Art students typically avoid lectures and essay-writing when they can, partly perhaps because the teaching and learning styles are too reminiscent of school. There is a resistance to the cultural breadth which wide reading and an open attitude to other disciplines would provide; a resistance to theory of all kinds; and a reliance on a tradition of visual, intuitive solutions which are not based on any form of textual research. This characteristic is clear in the literature. Gill, for example, as a seminal 20th century typographer who typically relies on sensitivity and traditional knowledge and whose writings are often recommended to students, brushes aside the findings of research: 'The readable may seem to be a measurable quality, verifiable by eyesight tests &

rational exposition; and this may be so; but the pleasantly readable is obviously a much more difficult matter...'[8] Sixty years later, a handbook of design for desktop publishing[17] comments on the inter-relationship between line-length and line-spacing but makes no reference to any objective research (such as[36]), nor indicates any sources of the author's knowledge – he is simply citing tradition and is typical in doing so. It is ironic that art and design institutions typically see themselves as radical and yet their reliance on traditional practice and modes of thought is second to none.

A culture of egoism

One of the major advantages of an art school training, as against some other educational methods, is the licence it gives students to constructively externalise their own ideas and emotions. But the price is that a culture of egoism emerges in which the only relationship deemed of value is between the student and his or her own work. Many art students see working with others as involving only regrettable compromises, not fruitful interactions.

A short report on the work of the Council for National Academic Awards in 1972 offered a checklist of 14 desirable topics for college courses. It included: problem-solving by logical methods; innovation and creativity; analysis and synthesis; and aesthetic appreciation. There were no remarks about team working.[25] Ten years later a handbook for intending art students mentioned in passing that 'designers have to learn to work with other people involved in the production process' and includes 'the ability to get on with people'. However, it devoted far more of its commentary to 'the capacity to believe in yourself and your ideas' and making 'personal responses'.[9] Another introduction to art school methods characterised the work as 'students [learn] to explore their own potential' and used the expressions 'individuality of approach and expression', 'creativity of the individual', 'personal exploration of the individual's creative ideas', again with no mention at all of group work.[32] A similar book in 1997 covers 'researching and developing ideas' and 'originating and developing ideas' entirely in the framework of individual activity.[18]

The scientific approach

In the alternative context of Computer Science, the study of human-computer interaction (HCI) has very different characteristics. A comprehensive attempt by an industry-education partnership to define curricula for the subject was made in 1992.[10] Components included psychology and cognitive science, sociology, statistics and the design of experiments, as well as information design and visual thinking. HCI students are expected to be in command of a wide range of analytical techniques, which are derived from existing work in the objective evaluation of human interaction with systems and are described in an extensive literature of books, journals and conference proceedings. Conference literature is dominated by papers reporting quantitative assessments made under experimental conditions. There is little emphasis on creativity but much on learning from the research undertaken by others.

Manuals of user interface design such as those by Shneiderman[33] and Thimbleby[35] are very different from the literature of art and design: there is a recognition that the success of a design incorporates objective as well as subjective responses; a respect for the research work of others; and above all an interest in objective methods of evaluation, to which both authors devote considerable space and by which their whole approach is informed. HCI specialists would be astonished to discover that these methods are largely unknown in art schools: to take a single example, most 'information design' in art schools is tested on no one, while any project on an HCI course would be considered essentially incomplete if it did not involve testing on typical subjects and thorough evaluation of the results.

Don Norman[23] commands respect in HCI circles for his writings on design, which are rooted in the detailed study of human behaviour in relation to technological devices, including extensive work on the phenomena of human errors ranging from the misunderstanding of photocopiers to the crashing of aeroplanes. His books are highly readable, almost entertaining, and yet many art students are completely unaware of them. Edward Tufte's books [38, 39, 40] combine an 'artistic' sensitivity to the visual with a 'scientific' intellectual curiosity and a willingness to study other people's research. He is largely unknown to design students, while he is extensively cited in the HCI world.

Problems with the scientific approach

The avid curiosity about the world which is the basis of the scientific method, is surely relevant to any form of design. It is vitally important that we should understand what users actually do with the products and prototypes which we devise. For example, there is no point in launching on an unsuspecting public a product which defies what is known about the laws of perception (and yet this happens all the time!). The greatest strength of the science approach lies in its curriculum, in which a huge wealth of information is provided to students, normally in a highly structured form, making them aware of a range of conceptual and technical techniques, principally of analysis and observation. Yet this strength also contains the germ of a weakness, emphasising as it does the analysis of *what already exists*, rather than what *might be brought into existence*. And above all, problems lie in regarding the specification of a learning strategy as lying principally in the curriculum, without regard for the systemic aspects of the process.

Some problems in HCI education have been identified by HCI specialists themselves. They include a poor take-up of ideas by industry and a dearth of experiential learning. There is also an inadequate fit of the overall educational package with the broad nature of Design, an issue we will need to look at in some depth.

Poor adoption by industry

Carroll[3] has identified problems with the predominantly evaluative nature of HCI studies. He has criticised much HCI work as being too laboratory-based and insufficiently concerned with real work in real-life contexts. He has also pointed out the poor takeup of HCI findings in industrial software development. In fact there is a widespread feeling in the HCI community that interface designers are brought in to fix problems which would not have arisen in the first place had interaction designers been consulted earlier and at a more basic level.

These two problems are surely related: the poor industrial take-up arises from a perception among software developers that HCI is too concentrated in the area of evaluation, at the expense of production: that it is essentially a reactive, 'academic' discipline and not a productive one. In short, there is a perception that a Human Factors specialist cannot tell you what you should do, only what you should *not* do.

This problem is significant for many design disciplines other than HCI: it arises particularly where both 'scientific' and 'artistic' design methods are on offer. Hillier[11] has commented on the relationship between science and innovation in architecture: 'What is governed by [scientific] laws is not the form of individual buildings but the field of possibilities within which the choice of form is made'...'Although in key respects [architecture's] forms can be *analysed and understood* by scientific means, its forms can only be *prescribed* by scientific means in a very restricted sense' (my emphasis). And Gill was perhaps making a similar point in the quotation already cited: 'The readable may seem to be a measurable quality... but the pleasantly readable is obviously a much more difficult matter...'. We could almost say that Art and Design tends to add to the range of possible designs—it grows additional branches on the tree – while Science tends to reduce them—it prunes out the unproductive, unsafe or unhealthy growth. Following this metaphor, we would be wise to remember that nourishing a tree and pruning it are equally necessary to its productiveness and well-being.

Lack of experiential learning

In contrast to the open-ended, project-based learning of the art school, Computer Science courses are dominated by the academic methods of lecture, tightly controlled 'practical' and examinations. Now it is clearly the case that formal examinations do have a place in some design disciplines, especially where the profession involves issues of public safety and liability. It is reasonable to insist on an objective test of a designer's knowledge if the designer is to create an artefact or system on which life depends. But surely for the great majority of design work examinations have no useful role. What matters is what students can do when faced with a brief, the available resources and a period of time in which to create their solutions, not what texts they can formulate from memory under artificial conditions.

Most HCI courses include one or more practical projects but these are seldom regarded as the core of the course and in many cases one practical project is regarded as enough to give the students an idea of what project development is all about. But to give form to ideas is a complex skill which requires substantial practical experience. Perhaps there is an assumption that this skill can be easily acquired, that it 'comes naturally'. It is true that it cannot easily be taught, but it can certainly be *learned*. This is a key objective of the art school regime, to provide repeated, intensive, practical experience in this most difficult of skills.

The idea of the usable tool

I implied earlier that the art school model of design is seriously incomplete in that it generally omits objective factors and has a romantic adherence to subjectivity. However, the shortcomings of the 'scientific' model will also become evident, misrepresenting both design and the process of designing.

To some, the word 'design' denotes a functional, engineering approach. To others it may mean styling—adding an attractive surface to a system whose functions have been defined by others. Most HCI literature implicitly or explicitly regards interactive products as tools. This is understandable for two reasons. First, to consider a product as a tool is to highlight the key issues of whether it works and whether it is usable by its intended users. Second, historically the great majority of computer-delivered products has been of a utilitarian kind. It is only in recent years that games, multimedia titles, enhanced CD-audio discs, promotional web-sites and other non-utilitarian interactive products have begun to demand serious consideration.

The tool metaphor leads to a simplistic view of designing as functional engineering, neglecting its potential role as a cultural, social and creative activity. It implies that the process is essentially one of problem-solving. This 'form follows function' view is exemplified in the famous remark of Corbusier that a house is a machine for living in (though in fact Corbusier did not hold a simple functionalist view). It assumes that effective designing is the correct determination of a solution based on the definition of the requirements: in short that it is a *selecting, filtering* or *narrowing* process. It also assumes a simplistic model of the reception of the designed artefact, where functional usability precludes the addressing of a wide range of human needs.

Many have questioned the functionalist approach. Lansdown[15] has pointed out that the 'brief', the attempt to catalogue the functions which a design must serve, is itself a part of the design and cannot be an exhaustive, objective account. Pye[29] shows that there are far too many solutions left, even after all the possible functional arguments have been used to narrow the range of solutions – the designer's intention is still a deciding factor. And Baxandall[1] has explored the complexity of the social, commercial and other influences which inevitably influence the form of designed artefacts.

Complementing the functionalist model of designing is an equally erroneous view of the role of the designed artefact. If we consider some non-computer artefacts, it is clear that many do indeed have a functional purpose (or several purposes) but their form is by no means limited to functional considerations: we need only think of newspapers or of clothes, both artefacts with a clear functional purpose. Clothes must normally keep us warm and dry, yet this tells us almost nothing about the form of the myriad different garments which are worn. Legibility in the design of a newspaper is presumably a prerequisite, yet the reason why one newspaper looks different from another is not to do with legibility or even readability but rather with the associative qualities of the type-face, layout, proportion of picture to text and so forth. To confuse the minimal prerequisite of functionality with the overall purposes of design is clearly to mistake the part for the whole. One designer's account[19] of a recent project highlights the multi-faceted nature of design which the form-follows-function view cannot represent: a prototype information system for a major museum, it had to fulfil at least these functions: to allow the museum to understand the process of building an interactive system; to give curators an understanding of asset management (and sell the concept to the curators against a largely sceptical view); to allow evaluation of the database and the interface; to explore ways in which the museum could deliver such information on a local area network and on the Web; to allow educationalists, students and visitors to plan a trip to the museum depending on their interests and to find for the design company itself better ways of capturing images, both in 2D and 3D. Few of these requirements are limited to simple visual, aural or interaction design: together they make a complex web of social and procedural influences.

It is often the non-functional aspects which make the difference between the success or failure of alternative designs and this is an area which HCI has largely failed to address.[37] Designers must be able to deal with these ill-defined associative, cultural qualities as much as with the functional aspects and one theoretical framework for this aspect of design is provided by Design Semantics (for example, Krippendorf[13]). The question which Design Semantics aims to solve is: how can the design of a product *express* its functions. It does not assume that the form of an artefact will automatically be ideal or complete simply because it answers a set of functional requirements. It assumes that the potential meanings of the object also require intentional construction. It posits not only a user of the artefact but a perceiver too and goes beyond the concept of affordances popularised by Norman.[23] Whereas affordances help the user to see how to use a product at the level of detail, they do not enable the user to interpret it as a whole. Design Semantics considers what Krippendorf calls 'making sense of things': how 'we can tell the difference between a town hall and a filling station and "read" the symbolism of a corporate headquarters as in the past people read the symbolism of a gothic cathedral'.[6]

Beyond Design Semantics lies what we might call Design Semiotics – the ability of a design to be affective and allusive, to evoke clusters of associated ideas and images. Theoreticians throughout the 20th century have been perplexed by the choices that people make: that, for example, they might prefer furniture in a 'distinctly hideous taste'[26] to that of intellectually approved designers. Such failure of understanding arises from an inability to encompass the allusive, associative qualities of the designs that many people enjoy: for example, the reasons why they may choose a design which suggests a romanticised past time or a foreign land. It has taken the work of projects such as Household Choices at Middlesex University, which treats with respect the aspirations and sympathies of real people, to begin to reveal the 'richness and specificity of cultural forms as they figure in the practical art of living'.[28] Often the intellectual deprecation which faces popular designs is subjectivity disguised in objective terms: it is fine for a design to allude to the Bauhaus but not to a holiday in Torremolinos, yet this is seldom stated.

Pleasure

HCI educators are only just beginning to take an interest in this social and cultural context of their work.[27] One of the limitations of views such as Norman's is that they cannot account for the role of pleasure. Even design semantics does not explicitly deal with it. To say that a product is 'usable' is on the one hand an accolade, on the other very faint praise indeed. If a car were merely described as 'usable' we would not expect to get much pleasure from driving it. Certainly the prerequisite is that something is functional, usable, but we feel we should be able to expect more than that. Pleasure is ignored by functional design theory and HCI is no exception (in a representative selection of eight standard works on HCI the number of index references to Function was 46, but to Pleasure was nil).

I would suggest a pyramid of values from usable to enjoyable. At the foundations lies 'form follows function', where products are *merely* usable. Next we encounter the affordances approach where the form of the design aims to make clear the functions of the parts, relying principally on basic perception and cognition. Design semantics tries to give expressive form to products, relying on users' broader cultural knowledge. But even this does not encompass products which the user elects to use, prefers. At the peak of the scale, we need a richer design theory and design practice. This is the area in which Art and Design education has made a vital contribution, but often without the underpinning of core functionality and usability. Notoriously, the most exciting, desirable, attractive products often prove to be deficient in use.

There have been moves to redress the balance in favour of an honest acknowledgement of pleasure. Csikszentmihalyi[7] has anatomised the psychology of happiness and Nelson[22] exhorted software designers to learn by going to video-game arcades. Any design education which aims to produce effective practitioners does its students a disservice if it fails to deal with associative, cultural qualities as much as with the utilitarian and this is one of the most obvious weaknesses of an exclusively 'scientific' approach to education and to design.

Devising an educational strategy

In our test case, the education of the interaction designer, we seem obliged to choose between two opposed traditions, each in its own way inadequate. Vaguely, we could say that we need courses which combine the best of the two approaches but what exactly does this mean? Remedies can create as many problems as they solve. How are we to modify existing Art and Design practice in the light of our concerns, incorporating best practice from other disciplines, without damaging what is already done well?

I have already mentioned, in passing, the curriculum, teaching and learning methods and the form of assessment, but Laurillard[16] points out that there is a fourth aspect to any educational strategy: context. In what follows, this will prove one of the most significant aspects. However, we need to remember that changes to one aspect of a course may require changes to another in order to be effective. For example, changes to the curriculum will sometimes require changes to the assessment method. Likewise, a problem identified in the curriculum might be solved not by changing that curriculum itself but by a change in the context. Laurillard's classification is useful so long as we keep these mutual relationships in mind. Rather than discussing these issues in the abstract, I will illustrate them with a course which has been developed over the past seven years, the MA in Design for Interactive Media at Middlesex University. I hope readers whose main concern is undergraduate work will feel that these issues are equally relevant to them, as I believe they are.

Context – multidisciplinary intake

While context can be defined in institutional terms and is mainly so defined by Laurillard, the context which has the most immediate impact on the on-campus student is that of other students. A trivial solution to the problems raised by a monotechnic intake would be to recruit from a far wider range of disciplines. Such a proposal often brings fears that entrants will have insufficient design experience to cope with the demands of the course. After all, whenever Foundation courses are threatened, as they have been in the UK periodically for 20 years, the argument is advanced that students' experience of Art and Design is so poor at school that some sort of bridging activity is essential to get students to a point where bachelor's level work can be done effectively. The increasing emphasis of the UK National Curriculum for schools on a narrowly defined literacy and numeracy seems likely to make this problem worse. So it may indeed seem that accepting the 'visually illiterate' into design courses can only be damaging. But this view is wrong for two reasons. The first is it that it lapses back into regarding the Art and Design method of designing as the only one. I have tried to indicate that there are other models of design than that of the art school, which though equally incomplete on their own, have a great deal to offer. Skills of analysis and structured problem-solving, knowledge of human perceptual faculties, understanding of quantitative methods, ability to extract useful knowledge from the research writings – all these are valuable contributions to the gamut of design methods.

The second error is to ignore the huge potential for students to learn from each other. As soon as we stop mistaking teaching for learning we appreciate that one of the most powerful sources of education for each student is the background of other students. Emphasis shifts away from considering education as a relationship only between student and institution or student and lecturer, to a recognition of students' interaction with each other. The pattern of recruitment is not extraneous to the educational process: it is fundamental to it.

Curriculum – filling the gaps?

I identified the damaging problem of anti-intellectualism within art schools and contrasted it with the relative rigour of Science teaching. An obvious solution, but the wrong one, would be to institute a series of lectures by one or more specialists which act in a similar way to existing 'related studies' or 'contextual studies' series, whose subjects are currently almost entirely confined to socio-cultural matters. But we only have to consider this precedent to see the difficulty:

the defining characteristic of 'related studies' is that they are not related (by students at least) to anything which happens in the studio. Almost without exception, such studies are delivered on the more or less traditional model of students consuming lectures and texts and then having their knowledge measured by the production of more texts, an approach largely uninformed by the very strengths of the Art and Design practice alongside which it takes place and which is perhaps influenced by a desire for academic respectability and to satisfy the demands of validation committees.

We could add new kinds of literature to our booklists and new forms of knowledge to the curriculum but if these activities are not embedded into the normal practice of studio work then their value will be largely wasted and may be begrudged by studio staff. Here is an example of a problem in one aspect of educational strategy which can be largely solved by altering a different aspect: the narrow-mindedness and inadequacy in the range of design strategies which are typical of the art school may seem to be problems of curriculum but their solution lies not principally with adding lectures on other methods of design but with changes to the context. At Middlesex we have had very limited success in covering these new areas by adding new lectures. What has begun to work is embedding advice on other (often more 'scientific') kinds of research into individual and group tutorials. We also try to ensure that theoretical and practical work is led by the same staff, in the same context, and even in the same physical location, as practical instruction. Seminars involve non-design lecturers in group critiques of practical work. As a result, we are starting to have some effect on the way our students approach the process of design. Once again, multidisciplinary recruitment is also a benefit, since all students meet those who have a stronger intellectual grounding than is traditional for the art student.

Teaching and learning – collaborative group work

Ramsden has said: 'The aim of teaching is simple: it is to make student learning possible.'[30] Project-based learning puts the student's own work at the centre of the learning process so that the teaching serves the needs of the project-work, not simply itself. An interesting difference between art school and science-based projects lies in the nature of the brief. Where projects are used on Science-based courses, they are always goal-oriented: the brief specifies what the result should be. An alternative is to allow open projects which are 'data-driven', where students can learn and innovate by exploring what a technology does. This resembles more the approach of Fine Art courses, where it is standard practice to explore media and techniques as a principal source of ideas. It resembles Klee's concept of 'taking a line for a walk'[12]: this open-ended approach is particularly necessary if we are to populate the design space with new ideas in the hope of extending the boundaries of the possible.

Even where project-based learning is the norm, there is a long-standing resistance to the full implementation of group, collaborative projects. In Science departments such approaches are undermined by the approach to assessment (dealt with below), while in Art and Design the obstacle is the obsession with individual self-development. Work at Middlesex has demonstrated that the range and depth of ideas is greater where cooperative work is encouraged, especially in a cross-disciplinary environment. Teamwork also reflects industry practice and the complex social nature of design: this surely is a case where nothing is gained by artificially constraining individuals to work alone. On Middlesex's MA course, not only have staff, external examiners and students all found diversity of recruitment very valuable, it has had a significant effect on the quality of the projects. It is worth illustrating this point: one particularly successful recent project was made by three students with backgrounds in graphic design, product design and nuclear physics, while another was by four students from backgrounds in investment finance, experimental psychology, illustration and communication theory. Such mixtures are typical. Considerable benefits also arose from the fact that these students brought to the course very different cultural perspectives, coming as they did from UK, Australia, Germany, Columbia and Norway. Teamwork capitalises on the benefits of multidisciplinary recruitment and has been a significant factor in allowing our students to mature, to acquire new knowledge and to learn the skills of talking and working with those from other backgrounds, disciplines and cultures.

Assessment – the final integration

I discussed the mutual relationship between the parts of an educational strategy. The form of assessment must always complement a curriculum and a curriculum cannot be devised without considering it. It must also reinforce the teaching and learning methods, not undermine them. There is no point in devising a course supposedly committed to project work if this is contradicted by the assessment methods. To base the learning on projects but then to assess by exam paper would defeat the object. The incorporation of the best aspects of science-based teaching such as evaluation and objective methods does not need to be accompanied by the dead hand of the traditional examination.

The form of assessment must match the course philosophy in other respects. Many modular courses use averaged marking schemes which reward students more or less equally for every part of their study. But does this fit with what we want from students? If the students are to innovate, they must be free to take risks. Developing our approach to assessment, we should take care that students are free to try an ambitious experiment, which may be unsuccessful, without failing the programme overall. At Middlesex, successful completion of the first semester allows admission to the second, and so on, but it is only the final semester which dictates the level of the final award: postgraduate diploma, MA, or MA with Distinction. Students must never feel that in order to end up with a good average they would be safest to study something they already know, or should take a conservative approach to the development of a project for fear of damaging their final grades.

Finally, assessment must also reflect group work. There are courses where group-based projects are nominally encouraged at some stages, only to be discouraged in the final assessed work. The construction of an appropriate marking scheme for group work requires careful thought. In our case it is done by allocating two equally weighted marks for each project to each student: one is a mark which they share with the other members of their project team, the other represents their personal contribution. So individuals benefit from being involved in a good project, and suffer from a bad one, but also have an opportunity to distinguish themselves (or disgrace themselves) within the group. In addition, one of the assessment criteria is group work, allowing us to specifically reward those who have worked in an open, cooperative, collaborative way.

There is no point in engineering changes in context (by multidisciplinary recruitment), in curriculum (by adopting a wider range of models of design) and in teaching and learning methods (by focusing on the benefits of project-based group work) if these changes are not part of an integrated solution fully reflected in both assessment criteria and assessment methods.

Acknowledgements

The ideas in this chapter were developed through work and conversation with several colleagues to whom my thanks are due. I would particularly like to acknowledge the contribution of Gordon Davies, co-founder of the MA Design for Interactive Media.

77

References

1   Baxandall, M. *Patterns of Intention – on the Historical Explanation of Pictures*, Yale University Press 1985

2   Blattner, M.M. and Dannenberg, R.B. (eds.). *Multimedia Interface Design*, ACM Press/ Addison-Wesley 1992, p.xviii

3   Carroll, J M (ed.). *Designing Interaction* Cambridge University Press 1991, p.1

4   Clayton, S., Davies G. and Hammersley, P. 'Progress in developing the discipline of Electronic Publishing' in Dyson, M. (ed.) *Teaching Electronic Publishing '94: Proceedings of the Workshop* April 12-13 Darmstadt, Germany (1994)

5   Cohen, B. *Educational Thought*, Macmillan and Co, London 1969, p.74-92

6   Crampton-Smith, G. (g.crampton-smith@ RCA.AC.UK) 'What is a designer?' contribution to email discussion list VISUAL-L@VTVM1.CC.VT.EDU Sun, 09 Feb 1997

7   Csikszentmihalyi, M. *Flow – the psychology of happiness*, Rider 1992

8   Gill, E *Essay on Typography*, Lund Humphries 1931 (fifth edition 1988), p.93

9   Green, P. *Working in Art and Design* Batsford (1983)

10 Hewett, T Baecker, R Card, S Carey, T Gasen, J Mantei, M Perlman, G Strong, G and Verplank, W *ACM SIGCHI Curricula for Human-Computer Interaction* Report of the ACM SIGCHI Curriculum Development Group, ACM: New York (1992)

11 Hillier, B. *Space is the Machine* Cambridge University Press 1996

12 Klee, P. *Pedagogical Sketchbook* (originally published as Pädagogisches Skizzenbuch, Germany 1925), Faber and Faber, London 1953

13 Krippendorf, K. 'On the essential contexts of artefacts or on the proposition that "Design is making sense (of things)"' in *Design Issues* vol. V, No. 2 Spring 1989

14 Lansdown, J. *Using the computer to augment creativity: computer choreography*, CEA Working Paper presented to International Symposium on Creativity and Cognition, Loughborough 1993

15 Lansdown, J. 'Commoditie, firmness and delight: what can software engineers learn from other designers?' in *Computer Bulletin* vol. 3 Part 4 December 1987, p. 4–7

16 Laurillard, D. *Rethinking University Teaching*, Routledge 1993

17 Lichty, T. *Design Principles for Desktop Publishers*, Scott, Foresman 1989 p.54

18 Lowry, P. *The Essential Guide to Art and Design*, Hodder and Stoughton 1997

19 McGirr, D. (personal communication) notes on a project undertaken by Diverse Interactive, London 1997

20 Marvin, C. *When old technologies were new*, Oxford University Press 1988

21 Musser, C. *Before the Nickelodeon*, University of California Press 1991, p.7

22 Nelson, T.'The right way to think about software design' in Laurel, Brenda (ed.) *The Art of Human-Computer Interface Design*, Addison Wesley 1990, p.235–243

23 Norman, D. *The Psychology of Everyday Things*, Basic Books, New York 1988

24 Oren, T. 'Designing a new medium' in Laurel B. *The Art of Human-Computer Interface Design*, Addison-Wesley 1990

25 Osborne-Moss, J. 'The Council for National Academic Awards' in *A report on Design in the Middlesex Polytechnic 1972/3*, Middlesex Polytechnic 1973

26 Pevsner, N. *An Enquiry into Industrial Art in England*, Cambridge University Press, (1937) p209

27 Portigal, S. 'Design as a cultural activity' in *SIGCHI Bulletin* 29, 3 1997 p.1214

28 Putnam, T. 'Design, Consumption and Domestic Ideals', Introduction to Putnam, Tim and Newton, Charles (eds.) *Household Choices*, Futures Publications and Middlesex Polytechnic, London 1990 p.7–19

29 Pye, D. *The Nature and Aesthetics of Design* Herbert Press 1978

30 Ramsden, P. *Learning to Teach in Higher Education*, Routledge 1992

31 Roe, A. *The Making of a Scientist*, Dodd Mead, New York 1952

32 Saxton, C. (ed.). *Art School*, Macmillan 1981

33 Shneiderman, B. *Designing the User Interface* (2nd edn.), Addison-Wesley 1992

34 Shneiderman, B. 'Education by engagement and construction: a strategic education initiative for a multimedia renewal of American education' in Barrett, Edward (ed.). *Sociomedia – Multimedia, Hypermedia and the Social Construction of Knowledge*, MIT 1992) p.13–26

35 Thimbleby, H. *User Interface Design*, ACM Press/Addison-Wesley 1990

36 Tinker, M. *Legibility of Print*, Iowa State University Press 1964

37 Tractinsky, N, 'Aesthetics and apparent usability: empirically assessing cultural and methodological issues' in *Proceedings of CHI '97* (Atlanta, GA, USA, March 22-27, 1997) ACM, New York 1997, p.115–122

38 Tufte, E. *The visual display of quantitative information*, Graphics Press, Connecticut 1983

39 Tufte, E. *Envisioning information*, Graphics Press, Connecticut 1990

40 Tufte, E. *Visual Explanations: images and quantities, evidence and narrative*, Graphics Press, Connecticut 1997

designing women: gender issues in graphic design education

Erica Matlow

Erica Matlow worked for many years as a practising graphic designer before moving into higher education. She has an MA from the Institute of Education in the Sociology of Education and is currently researching for her PhD entitled 'The impact of new technologies on graphic design education'. She is course coordinator for the Graphic Information Design BA (Hons) and a principal lecturer at the University of Westminster in the School of Communication, Design and Media. She co-ordinates 'Cutting Edge' the Women's Research Group and is co-editor of two 'Cutting Edge' books, 'Desire by Design' and 'Digital Dreams'. She is co-vice chair of CADE (Computers in Art and Design Education), on the editorial advisory board of 'Digital Creativity' and a fellow of the RSA (Royal Society of Arts).

Introduction

Dale Spender asserts that:

> *The world of computers and their connections is increasingly the world of men: as more research is done in this new area and more findings are presented, the more damning is the evidence. Men have more computers, spend more time with them, and are the dominating presence in cyberspace. Considering its roots are sunk deep in academia and the military-industrial complex, that's hardly surprising.*[8]

In this chapter I will be measuring Spender's assertion against the changes that have taken place in the working lives of two women lecturers, MH who teaches on a Graphic Information BA course, and BW who taught on a Visual Communication BA course. Specifically, I will be exploring the relationship that these women have had with computers in teaching graphic design and how they have experienced and negotiated the paradigm shift from mechanical print to the electronic screen. I will also be contextualising their related experiences within the broader context of graphic design education.

Gender issues

> *Men and women in our society have very different experiences in nearly every aspect of their lives, so it is not surprising to find that their experiences with respect to technology are also very different. Boys and men are expected to learn about machines, tools and how things work. In addition, they absorb ideally, a 'technological world view' that grew up along with industrial society. Such a world view emphasises objectivity, rationality, control over nature and distance from human emotions. Conversely, girls and women are not expected to know much about technical matters. Instead, they are to be good at interpersonal relationships and to focus on people and on emotion. They are to be less rational, less capable of abstract, 'objective' thought.*[1]

82

Both MH and BW acknowledge that they are not technically minded and it is not unusual for women to be antipathetic to technology in general for reasons illustrated by the quote above. Dale Spender's earlier assertion should then be challenged, as women have shown that they can be as technically aware and as skilled as their male counterparts but perhaps are simply making different choices in relation to communications technology. Kirkup points to the diminishing number of women who choose computing as a career and suggests that there is 'a spiral of increasingly male industry developing an increasingly masculine technology'.[5]

Although, as previously stated, BW believes that gender conditioning at an early age has created the difficulties that many women encounter in their understanding of technology, she is also aware that some of her younger female colleagues have moved beyond the restraints of this conditioning and take a pride in fully understanding technology, especially when it is in a male dominated area. 'These women believe it to be really important that they are seen to be technically proficient as it imbues them with more credibility in a male dominated profession.'[14] It is certainly apparent that women experience additional pressures when working in a typically male-oriented environment, they have to work harder than men, are more committed and become more involved with the students at an interpersonal level.

Turkle suggests that gender conditioning can be modified and believes that feminists should feel optimistic about the potential effect of computers in society. She identifies the different ways that men and women form attachments with their computers and the different styles they adopt when working with them. Women are seen as more connected with their machines, whilst men adopt a more 'distanced stance, planning, commanding and imposing principles on them'. This work by Sherry Turkle [9,10] is considered by Kirkup and Keller to be important in addressing some of the 'deeper reasons why many women do not enjoy computing'.[5]

Turkle's early research looked at the relationship of adults and children to their computers. She identified two different styles of relating, one she called 'hard' mastery which was premised on a control, 'a style more comfortable with formal hierarchical programming techniques...'[9] The other style was 'soft' mastery, the process of negotiating with computers usually adopted by women and girls. The acquisition of these skills, differentiated by gender are, according to Turkle, acquired at an early stage of infancy when the development of the child is still closely bound into the mother–child relationship. The separation of child from the mother is the point at which she or he experiences the world 'out there' and develops a sense of objective reality. It is also the point at which the child becomes gendered. Turkle believes that the particular Oedipal boy/mother relationship results in the boy preferring distanced objective relationships whilst girls feel easier with 'the pleasures of closeness with other objects as well'.[9]

The concept of science as an objective tradition and as the typical male preserve can be seen to be built, therefore, on men's earliest experience of object relationships. Girls have a more continuous relationship with their mothers which then enables them to develop a different sense of themselves and 'other', to develop a 'softer' relationship to the 'hard' male world of science. This traditional division of gender into 'hard' = male and 'soft' = female is certainly problematic in that it continues to support the status quo and, as we have seen, reduces a complex range of issues into a simple binary set of oppositions but it can be a useful concept with which to encourage a less biased approach to the teaching of computing skills to women.

In later research posited on the work of the educational psychologist Piaget, Turkle develops the concept of 'bricolage' instead of 'soft' mastery and a formal analytical approach instead of 'hard' mastery. Bricolage can be seen as a useful concept because it opens up the potential for creative computing. It enables associations to be made where you can 'start with one idea, associate to another and find a connection with a third'.[9] This is a far more flexible, interactive and connected approach than the formal, analytical, distanced approach associated with the male computer culture, which is also dominantly white, western and middle-class.

MH describes how, over the last three years, she has met many highly computer literate women students who arrive on the course as well as men 'who arrive on the course as 100% nerds'. But although she has also encountered some women students who were still fearful of the technology, she genuinely believes that the gender differences are not so great.

Sherry Turkle believes that one of the reasons women are alienated from the computer culture is that 'the present social construction of programming styles and computer culture encourages one particular style of thinking which is not only repressive for many women, but restricts the potential of computers'. She feels that it is important to develop a comfortable relationship with a computer in order to feel happy about working with one. This experience was borne out by the respondents in 'Women, computers and a sense of self' when detailing the, mainly positive, relationships with their own personal computers.

The questionnaire

In my initial research for this chapter I asked the two women, MH and BW, to respond to a short questionnaire and to specifically focus on the personal experiences they have had with computers and on their relationship with communication technologies in their work as graphic design lecturers. In addition, I have had access to the graphic design course documents from four universities, covering the period 1978 to the present, and have drawn on these to supplement, contextualise and extend the more personal responses of the questionnaire.

The women were asked to formulate their responses in the shape of a dialogue rather than with yes or no answers. The intention was to explore, from the personal perspectives of both respondents, how the graphic design courses had accommodated and integrated the computer into their curriculum. Also what kind of impact this might have had on the individual courses and on the lecturers own 'sense of self' and attitude to teaching. I have also drawn on two other small scale case studies, 'Women, Computers and a Sense of Self',[6] which I conducted earlier this year and 'Disciplinary Discourses: a case study of gender in information technology and design courses'.[2]

The questionnaire was divided into five sections: First Experiences, New Kinds of Learning, Curriculum Change, Gender Issues and Future Visions. In 'First Experiences' I asked about the womens' initial relationship with computers, when they first started to teach with computers and the sort of access that was made available to their students. I wanted to know what kind of computers they used and if they were given any encouragement to use them as an integral component of their work. In the second section 'New Kinds of Learning' I wanted to know how both women felt about the way computers were introduced onto their course and whether they were given any staff development in their use. The third section 'Curriculum Change' asks both women whether they had experienced any difficulties teaching the new communication technologies and what changes had occurred as a result of the incorporation of the computers into the curriculum. In section four 'Gender Issues' the focus is more on understanding their specific gendered experience and relating this to the broader issues of gender conditioning in the area of computing education. 'Future Vision', the last section, raises issues around the convergence of new media and the possible loss of skills associated with the older, more traditional graphic design practices.

First experiences

This section looks at the way that computing technology was introduced onto both women's graphic design courses and the impact this has had on the courses and the individual experiences of the women themselves. Traditionally, graphic design education has been involved with teaching design and production for print-based media focusing on the integration of type and image. This has also meant, at times, the incorporation of photography, illustration, animation and video. This discourse was radically transformed and its practice changed with the introduction of the new technologies onto degree courses in the late 1980s. Until this time very few graphic design degree courses possessed computer technology for teaching computer graphics, though BW's university with its commercial investment in 'state of the art' hardware and software was one of the first colleges to introduce computing into its design curriculum. MH's course only acquired a specific network of 'art and design' Macintosh computers in 1989, though previously students had access to 'typing' and word processing on basic Amstrad computers supplied and taught by the Business department.

MH's first experiences, with IBM computers in 1985, were extremely frustrating involving her in highly complex procedures and systems. She was then introduced to the Apple Mac, when, as stated above, a network of computers was purchased for use by staff and students. The technician arranged staff development workshops but though MH attended she was never that involved. The students were inducted into the computer network by the same technician and were, she says, encouraged to use them 'as part of their everyday graphic design education', as another part of their design 'tool kit'.

Even though her early experiences with computing were so disappointing the introduction of Macintosh computers encouraged MH to buy her own Mac Classic for domestic use in the early 1990s which she replaced with a Power Mac 6100 in 1995. These were purchased mainly for their word processing capabilities and their educational programmes, to support her sons' homework, though MH mentions that her sons also used them to play computer games on. In the mid 1980s L. Culley[3] conducted a survey of English schoolchildren and observed that when a computer was bought for home use it was most likely to be used almost exclusively by the males in that household, almost entirely for game-playing.

In the mid 1980s, although her university did possess 'state of the art' computing facilities, BW remembers that there was only 'isolated use of the computers for teaching graphic design'. This situation had occurred, she felt, because most of the staff, at this time, had 'not got their head around computers' and also that staff and students only had limited access to them for personal staff development.

BW learnt to use a computer by borrowing a Macintosh from the Graphic Design department and working her way through a 'step by step' manual over a holiday period. Learning through doing was also the preferred method of most of the respondents in 'Women, computers, and their sense of self'[3] who said they were largely self-taught either from manuals, or from watching other people, although Dale Spender[8] believes that most women were probably taught to use a computer by 'one of their female friends'. The respondents also added that their initial experiences with a computer were often 'frustrating and unfriendly' or 'frightening' until, that is, they were introduced to a Macintosh computer. When asked whether learning to use the computer was a good or bad experience, BW found working with a computer was exciting but that some aspects, like programming, were frightening and she certainly did not want to get involved in the inner workings of her machine. She also felt that the more technical aspects of computing should be 'someone else's responsibility'.

Like BW , the respondents in 'Women, computers, and their sense of self'[6] also found the internal workings of the computer problematic; some were over-awed by the invisibility of the works, by the machine's 'physical opacity',[10] others found the computer 'alienating at first' but later it became more 'familiar and reassuring'. One woman compared her computer to a car: she describes both as tools which should be as transparent as possible. This suggests that she was happy to be able to manipulate the surface simulations of her computer without becoming involved with the machine at any deeper level. Continuing the analogy between car and computer, she would certainly not want to encourage the fantasy that she could just 'open the hood and see inside'.[10] Although most of the women in both studies had initial similar negative experiences when first confronted with computing technology, this reluctance was usually short lived as they became more computer dependent and the computer became more central to their individual development and work activities.

BW attributes her difficulty in understanding the 'mechanics' of technology to her gender conditioning. Though, as S. Clegg et al[2] describe, the relationship of the technical to masculinity embraces too many complex conceptualisations to be reduced to the simple binary formula of masculine and feminine. BW felt that her inability to come to grips with how technology worked was a disadvantage to her at work but believed that most of her other colleagues, male or female, did not feel the same way.

Recent research[15] though does indicate that for most women their initial experiences of working with a computer have not been that favourable. S. Clegg et al state that 'Women mostly came into computing through various types of work experience or through school which suggests that girls have already had experiences which confirm computing as a gendered discourse...as "guests" in the "hosts" boys' space.' The authors also state that their women respondents experienced their school computing as a place 'where dominant boys claim expertise'.[2]

New kinds of learning

As we have seen in the previous section, both BW and MH developed their relationship with computers at a relatively late stage in their careers. Both came into teaching in the 1960s and would be considered by Spender[8] to be the last generation 'reared within a culture in which print is the primary information medium'. The women had grown up and become skilled in a print-based community and had developed certain ways of making sense of their world through print. To this extent they were what print had made them and, according to Spender, because of new communication technologies they now were facing the need to change.

Certainly, the massive developments that have taken place in communication technology have changed many aspects of the way the women are now able to communicate. It has opened up new ways of working, created new communities of interest, new kinds of relationships real and virtual, and provided new roles and new identities. BW was interested in how the computer worked, to know what the computer could enable her to do and how she could use it to extend her own creativity. She gives as an example her design of a magazine double-page spread.[12]

This innovative typographic layout with its layered text and abutting headlines was considered at the time to be unreadable by her peers but was influential in starting the trend for 'deconstructed' typography.[16]

MH was reluctant to get involved with the new Macs, owing perhaps to a lack of motivation, and believed that they were just another extension to the existing graphics 'tool kit', whereas BW was excited by the potential the Macs offered to break with established modernist design conventions. MH also felt reluctant to openly express her 'addiction to and confidence in the Mac' because she believed that this might have antagonised the other staff. BW felt that for some of her colleagues the introduction of computing into the design curriculum was intimidating as it challenged preconceived conventions and established ways of working. Other staff though saw the computer as enabling, with the potential to transform a whole range of social issues, cultural forms and modes of practice.

BW believed that computers were initially introduced into the graphic design course in a rather piecemeal way as 'different staff took to them at different rates'. Computers have therefore only really become an established component of the graphic design curriculum over the last four or five years as staff become more competent and confident in their use. It has now become established practice, on both courses, to introduce students to computers via a general workshop before they are allowed open access to them, although, increasingly students come to degree education complete with sophisticated computer skills.

Curriculum Change

As well as running introductory computer skills workshops, both courses have undergone a period of rapid change and have had to adapt their course curriculum in order to incorporate the new communication technologies. For some courses these changes have occurred over a ten-year period but, as cited above, other courses have only started to change over the last four or five years. On MH's course Macs were introduced in 1990 and are now a centralised facility also constituting a central component of most course curricula in the school. This has led to a synergy and a merging of what, hitherto, have been highly specialised and specific course identities.

What have these changes meant to the staff who teach with and on the new technologies? Both staff and students now have to think about different ways of structuring and designing information as they now have to negotiate different kinds of 'graphic' spaces. Projects now are about the integration of moving images, sound, time, space, gesture and non-linear narrative which involves working in a virtual space as opposed to a flat two-dimensional one. This has meant, according to Steven Heller[4] that the designer's role has had to be redefined 'from (a) manipulator of form to (a) navigator of content'.

BW states that she enjoyed thinking 'virtually' and has found working with computers an exciting challenge. She states that the majority of the staff see the application of 'style' as 'both acceptable and desirable' but feels that she may have been prevented from having access to the third years because she was not interested in, and positively discouraged 'decoration' and style 'for the sake of it'. In a similar vein, MH also thinks that students can be seduced by the new media and produce work which is often superficial and gimmicky, relying on surface appearance rather than 'design thinking'. MH believes that making things by hand requires a 'different kind of thinking' than that required when you are working electronically. It means paying closer attention to detail and perhaps developing a greater degree of awareness at a more profound level.

The biggest difficulty MH experienced in working with students on the computer was again to do with a lack of confidence in understanding how the technology worked. She found it difficult to get beyond the technical problems and would revert to working with paper rather than wait for things to get fixed. She also found difficulty in gaining an overview of the students' work on screen unless they had provided some kind of visual map. When her course became more computer intensive, MH was inclined to defer to the two or three more technically proficient (male) members of staff. She remembers there being very little discussion, amongst the staff about 'computer issues' and if there was any discussion then the staff tended to divide into 'rival' camps: those that embraced the technology and those who were more resistant to it.

Future visions

MH identifies two major changes in her graphic design curriculum which have occurred since the introduction of computers. One is the interest of some staff in visual perception, cognition and the developments of A.I., and the other is the shift from print-based technologies to computer-based technologies. This shift from print to computer has had ramifications across most work activities of university staff and wrought changes not only in course design and curricula but in teaching, research and administration.

There has been a significant shift of focus from the book to the computer, bringing with it crucial changes both to staff members' identity as lecturers and, to some degree, their authority. 'The advent of the computer has upset traditional images of pedagogic authority...if education was once built on an apprentice system that included a careful mastery of tools, that system has been severely destabilised. Many students are now far more advanced in their control of their electronic tools than their instructors are.'[6]

As I have stated previously, both women have come into computing late in their lives and have had to work hard to keep up with the rapid change in technological developments. They have had to learn different skills and new ways of working in relation to the computer and in doing so have defined new roles and ways of working for themselves. Dale Spender talks about how the 'certain values that have served us well while we used print to make our world' can now actually be 'an obstacle – now that we are obliged to work with the new technologies'.[8,13] We are continually having to learn new skills; it doesn't stop with word-processing; we now have Email and the Net and 'for those of us who were reared with print, the continual effort to learn the new technologies will be an ongoing fact of life'.[8] This has certainly been the experience of MH, who recently has discovered the usefulness of email as an effective facility for communicating with her students and for giving mini tutorials.

Conclusion

In writing this paper I have drawn on the response from two women who both have considerable experience of graphic design education. I have also used material from two other case studies, which though small in scale, have clearly demonstrated the continuing tensions that exist in the world of computing for women. Two of the three case studies have been restricted to white middle-class women, though the third, by S. Clegg et al., have also included men. To pursue this research further, though, it would be necessary to broaden the study profile to include a much wider spectrum of respondents, in respect of ethnic origin, class and status within the educational hierarchy.

Both respondents, because of the nature of their work as lecturers in graphic design, have had to incorporate computers into their lives over a relatively short period of time, the last ten years. MH was initially reluctant to acknowledge their arrival and has been slower in accepting their integration onto the graphic design course, leaving the development and the acquisition of computer skills to the more (computer) motivated staff. BW, on the other hand, exhibited enthusiasm for computers when they were first introduced but is reluctant to get involved with their inner (technical) workings. MH expresses greater concerned about the loss of traditional graphic design skills than BW but is quick to recognise the need to incorporate new areas of knowledge into the curriculum that would develop a greater understanding of computer work. She is sceptical though about the potential of the computer, which she sees merely as a medium with which students can externalise their ideas. BW has expressed her involvement with the Macintosh computer as 'a form of addiction' and believes in the computer as a medium of expression as well as a design tool.

Both women say that they are reluctant to take any technical responsibility for the computer when they are teaching and would tend to refer to other (male) staff or technicians if problems occurred of a technical nature. This has created a different power relationship on the courses, with the 'technical' often taking precedence over the 'academic'. It also demonstrates the 'soft' mastery approach described by Turkle and supports, misguidedly, the commonly held assumption that women are technically incompetent. MH believes that while she may have been disadvantaged generally across all aspects of her work because of her gender she does not think that it has been any worse in relation to computers. BW, on the other hand, believes that she has been disadvantaged most specifically in the area of computing, because of her gender.

To refer to the quote by Benston that I used at the start of the section 'Gender Issues', girls, from a very early age, have an expectation that computers are really boys' toys and that girls are 'not expected to know much about technical matters'. In order to change this perception it is necessary to change the way computers, hardware and software, and computer design practices are gendered and to create different kinds of working and thinking spaces for the development of non-specific gendered computer practices. These spaces should be highly personalised and designed to suit the individual woman's needs and expectations and should be as far removed from the sterile environment of the traditional computer lab as possible.

We should also be encouraging a more 'participatory, non-hierarchical, and non-authoritarian approach'[7] to the design process itself. We should be encouraging women as far as possible to be more confident in their relationship to the computer because, as Turkle and Papert suggest, 'whether or not one enjoys working with a computer depends on developing a comfortable relationship with one'.[11] We could also encourage women to become 'bricoleurs', identified by Turkle earlier on in this chapter in the section 'Gender Issues' as this would enable them to be more connected to their work. We should be stressing the need for the computer to be considered a part of a social process of interaction with the user a primary component of this interaction as women are usually 'more comfortable with a relational, interactive and connected approach'.[11] than men, who generally prefer a 'more distanced stance, planning, commanding and imposing principles'.[11] In order then to implement this, women need to become more involved in their use of computers and to make greater demands of all future computing technology in relation to their own design activity.

References

1   Benston, M. 'Women's voices/men's voices: technology as language', Kirkup G and Keller L., (eds.). *Inventing Women: Science, technology and gender*, Polity Press in association with the Open University 1992

2   Clegg, S., Mayfield W., and Trayhurn D. 'Disciplinary Discourses: a case study of gender in information technology and design courses', *Gender and Education*, vol 11, no. 1, 1999

3   Culley, L. in 'The social construction of computers', Kirkup G., Kirkup G., and Kelly L., *Inventing Women: science, technology and gender.*, Polity Press in association with The Open University 1992

4   Heller S. *Masters of the Universe: Yale University School of Art Graphic Design Program*, Upper and Lower Case, vol. 22. no. 4 1996

5   Kirkup G., and Kelly L., *Inventing Women: science, technology and gender*, Polity Press in association with The Open University 1992

6   Matlow E. *Women, computers and a sense of self*, Cutting Edge, Digital Dreams, London and NY: I.B.Tauris., forthcoming March 2000

7   Levant de Brettville, S. 'Some Aspects of Design from the Perspective of a Woman Designer,'Bierut, M., Helfand, J., Heller, S., and Poyner, R., *Looking Closer, 3: Classic writings on Graphic Design*, Allworth Press, New York 1999

8   Spender, D. *Nattering on the Net*, Australia: Spinifex Press 1995

9   Turkle S. *The Second Self*, New York: Simon and Schuster 1984

10 Turkle S. *Life on Screen*, New York: Simon and Schuster 1995

11 Turkle, S. and Papert, S. 'Epistemological pluralism: styles and voices within the computer culture,' *Signs: Journal of Women in Culture and Society*, vol. 16, no.1, 1990 Kirkup G., and Kelly L., Inventing Women: science, technology and gender., Polity Press in association with The Open University 1992

12 Wilkins B. *Text and Image*, Octavo 7, June 1990

13 By 'us' and 'we' Spender is specifically referring here to women.

14 Quote from BW response to questionnaire.

15 The gendered acquisition of computing skills has already been been well-documented. See Turkle, S. *Life on Screen*, New York: Simon and Schuster, 1995 Lander R., and Adam, A. (eds) *Women in Computing*, Exeter Intellect Books 1997; Benyon, J. and Mackay, H. *Computers into Classrooms*, London Falmer Press 1993

16 The term 'deconstruction' was coined by the philosopher Jacques Derrida in the 1960s and entered into 'design culture as a stylistic category applied to architecture, products and graphics'. Lupton, E. and Abbott, J, Miller, 'History, Theory and Undergraduate Education', Heller, S., (ed.), *The Education of a Graphic Designer*, Allworth Press, New York 1980

what tangled webs we weave

Mike Hope

Mike Hope has recently been appointed as Associate Dean and Head of Exeter School of Arts & Design at the University of Plymouth. Prior to this he was course leader for Graphic Design at the Nottingham Trent University. He was a founder member of the ICOGRADA (International Council of Graphic Design Associations) Steering Committee for Archives and Research. From this arose the ARIADNE (Archival Retrieval Interface for Acknowledged Designer Network Exploration) software package/project which was used to record the life and work of eminent designers (eg FHK Henrion and WM de Majo). In addition he is a board member of a number of international and national organisations, such as the ISTD (International Society of Typographic Designers), the European Academy of Design and a member of the Editorial Board of its publication, The Design Journal. He has given papers at a number of international conferences on Multimedia/ Multimedia education and acts as an external examiner on a range of related graphics/multimedia programmes.

The digital revolution is all pervading and insidious in its march towards total domination, not just of the ways in which we communicate but of most aspects of our lives. It has, in the guise of the World Wide Web, delivered a system which is at once wonderful, seemingly boundless in its potential, anarchic in its lack of control and truly global in its operation and delivery. Historically it is just a continuation of an ongoing process of communications development which stretches back throughout human history.

> *The implementation of multimedia capabilities in computers is just the latest episode in a long series: cave paintings and hand-crafted manuscripts, the printing press, radio and television...These advances reflect the innate desire of man to create outlets for creative expression, to use technology and imagination to gain empowerment and freedom for ideas.*[5]

Its potential as a key tool for information exchange in the next decade is un-questionable. Its ability to be 'designed' in a globally effective and aesthetically acceptable way has yet to be answered. Historically, the great developments in communications have always overlapped, running alongside one another for a considerable time before the new process, borrowing heavily from its pre-decessor, superseded it.

> *The printed book also perpetuated, in the same forms but with greatly increased circulation, the success of genres established by the manuscript libellous...A second and powerful element rooted printed culture in the long time span. Well before the Gutenberg revolution, a new manner of reading – silently, using eyes alone – had broken with the oral reading that had long been universally obligatory (or nearly so)...With silent reading a new relation with writing was instituted, more private, freer, and totally internalized.*[3]

What we now see happening is not only the replacement of the static page with the electronic screen but the addition of moving image and sound. These develop-ments allow for a new level of freedom with respect to the manipulation of infor-mation into a truly multimedial interactivity.

So much of what is currently available on the Web appears to lack any structural or aesthetic considerations. Design as a discipline and the centuries of tradition seem to have been swept away or forgotten. It is, as yet, an unanswered set of questions for the burgeoning Web design/multimedia industry and the many design students who will take up their places in the vanguard of this sector of the design industry, as to whether there are or should be any new rules for Web design, to help achieve a global and aesthetically acceptable outcome.

> *Obviously, centuries of different forms of communication needn't be ignored. Rich lessons rest within diverse disciplines like typography, sequential art, and oral*

storytelling. But while other media can guide us, simply moving methods from one medium to another seldom works.The truly exhilarating Web sites are the ones that make you think "Wow this couldn't be done anywhere else but on the Web"...The Web for all its advantages, challenges designers, authors and engineers with cripplingly slow speeds, and archaic lack of typographic and layout control, and a cultural history rooted not in communication but in the obscure discipline of computer science...[9]

What will future students need for their toolkit, not just for survival but to ensure the ability to effectively work in and help push forward the whole area of Web design? Amongst the plethora of specialist courses, which continue to sprout at an alarming rate, just what is being delivered to the student? And is it relevant?

The Web is a vehicle for the dissemination of information in the form of text and images (both moving and still) and has the ability to utilise this information in the maximum possible number of ways. People choose and need information for a multitude of reasons and therefore approach its consumption and dissemination in what appears to be an endless set of permutations. Let me make an analogy. A trip into any large-scale newsagents or bookseller will, especially with periodicals and magazines, reveal the following scenario. You fight your way through masses of intently browsing readers. Material is being devoured, flicked through from the front, from the back, specific sections and articles read and so on. These magazines are collected into themed sections, which in turn have carefully thought out hierarchical strategies with regard to positioning, height, etc. You are, in short, and for a brief moment, living in a form of three dimensional Website. More often than not it is very frustrating, you cannot see clearly where a specific magazine is. Someone else is browsing through the only copy or what you want is not available, although plenty of alternative material is. You may not understand the positioning and layout of the section. All of this before you even get to the actual information. What is called for is a clear navigational structure to enable interactivity to take place.

The secret of clarity in Web design is to rigorously anticipate a user's process of discovery while eloquently and succinctly placing clues to your content in buttons, blurbs, and images across our site. Remember your audience is not coming to your Web site to see the interface. Visitors want to see the content. Show them what you've got and how to get there. Then get out of the way.[8]

To achieve this it is vital to grasp from the outset the importance of interactivity. It is the dissemination of information through one of four basic structural forms, namely: Linear, Hierarchical, Non-Linear and Composite.

Linear is the most basic sequential form of information provision.

Hierarchical is another familiar concept, with the structure appearing like a series of roots emanating from a central point but with little or no interaction between the roots.

Non-Linear appears, at first glance, seemingly organised chaos with material accessible to and from any given point.

Composite is the most complex system, allowing a combination of the previous three systems. Material is therefore accessible to and from any given point and, where necessary, utilises the employment of much more defined heirarchical and linear structures as and when required.

These four structures should form the starting point and basic building blocks in the design and construction of a website.

In the search for a new visual language there are eight existing clusters of key methodological vocabularies upon which to draw:

The Graphic Visual Language, Sound, Time and Movement, Cinematic Language, TV Language, Touch and Kinaesthesia, Words and, finally, Non Verbal Communication. Within each of these categories are a large number of elements, some of which overlap with other categories.

The graphic visual language

This has a massive historical tradition and, despite many different visual cultural interpretations, can be distilled down into basic forms such as line, tone, colour, shape, style, symbol, etc.

Sound

Once again this has a massive range of culturally diverse traditions upon which to draw and includes traditional musical language, everyday sounds, mechanical language and sounds, volume, pitch, timbre, position, stereo, etc.

Time and Movement

This vocabulary includes panning, tilting, tracking, sinking, rising, sprites, flashing, oscillating parallax, greying out, colouring, etc. and can be seen to have a lot in common with the next vocabulary, Cinematic language.

Cinematic language

This covers such subjects as genre, style and very specific filmic procedures such as styles of cuts, pulling focus, zoom, etc. As a genre it is barely one hundred years old and has in turn plundered other, older and traditional forms such as painting and theatre.

TV language

This is the youngest of the eight vocabularies. Like its near relation cinematic language, it draws heavily on all the other genres. Indeed, it overlaps almost completely with cinematic language but through the process of absorbtion and its unique needs, it has developed such specialities as talking heads, live outside broadcasting, opening sequences and commercial breaks.

Touch and kinaesthesia

This is perhaps the least understood and most under utilised of the vocabularies. Within this area are such issues as control of the computer mouse, control and positioning of buttons and/or roll-overs upon the screen. Increasingly the touch sensitive screen will become an important tool, as will speech recognition.

Words

This encompasses both the written and spoken word. The importance of para-linguistics cannot be stressed too highly, alongside the use of accents, grammar, specific vocabularies, tone, etc. Typographically speaking, the depiction and imbuing of a sense of meaning and emotion into words has rapidly expanded during the course of the last century.

Non-verbal communication

This utilises both iconic and actual representations of various gestures and facial expressions. It covers all forms of body language, for example, hand gestures.

It may seem surprising that a possible ninth methodological vocabulary, that of an ability to script and manipulate a number of computer languages such as HTML and Java, has not been included. Such is the speed of development that in just four years software programs have gone from immensely complex and off-putting applications to being the very latest code free-drag-and-drop packages (e.g. Dreamweaver 3) which allow whole websites to be built quickly and easily. These latest software applications will also ensure that the newly authored site is efficient in terms of size, allowing quicker downloading time and also taking care of net installation. This development, therefore, makes a detailed under-standing of computer scripting unecessary.

Many of these vocabularies are never fully considered or examined by designers and certainly do not form part of many syllabus. Paradoxically, the way forward in terms of web development lies in a full understanding of the role and function that these play in creating effective websites and indeed helping in the creation of the sense of emotion within websites.

Simplicity is absolutely essential on the Web. As our network world grows increasingly complex, layers and streams of information constantly bombard us. Successful Web design takes control of content and boils its presentation down to essential elements in a subtle visual context. You can achieve this by using cultural, virtual, and metaphorical contexts to say much more than you can by writing long explanations for everything on your pages. A careful mix of speed, technical prowess, and simplicity will make your designs more than just clear and understandable. It will enable you to push this new medium as far as it will go.[7]

All of the technological developments and the search for new coherent methodologies has supported the phenomonal growth, in barely 30 years, of hypertext. Sven Birkerts in his book *The Gutenberg Elegies – The fate of reading in an electronic age* sets out with a clarity the whole development of and reason for hypertext. He quotes from an article by Robert Coover:

Hypertext is not a system but a generic term, coined a quarter of a century ago by a computer popularist named Ted Nelson to describe the writing done in the nonlinear or nonsequential space made possible by the computer. Moreover, unlike print text, hypertext provides multiple paths between text segments, now often called 'lexias' in a borrowing from the pre-hypertextual but prescient Roland Barthes. With its webs of linked lexias, its networks of alternate routes (as opposed to print's fixed unidirectional page-turning) hypertext presents a radically divergent technology, interactive and polyvocal, favouring a plurality of discourses over definitive utterance and freeing the reader from by the author. Hypertext reader and writer are said to become co-learners or co-writers, as it were, fellow travellers in the mapping and remapping of textual (and visual, kinetic, and aural) components, not all of which are provided by what used to be called the author...[1]

Birkerts goes on to utilise provacative militaristic terminology to give more impact to his message and the sense of change:

Ground Zero: the transformation of the media of communication maps a larger transformation of consciousness – maps it, but also speeds it along, it changes the terms of our experience and our ways of offering response. Transmission determines reception determines reaction. Looking broadly at the way we live – on many simultaneous levels, under massive stimulus loads – it is clear that mechanical–linear technologies are insufficient. We require swift and obedient tools with vast capacities for moving messages through networks. As the tools proliferate, however, more and more of what we do involves network interaction. The processes that we created to serve our evolving needs have not only begun to redefine our experience, but they are fast becoming our new cognitive paradigm...[1]

An understanding of hypertext is therefore an essential pre-requisite of being able to engage in any constructive multimedial dialogue, let alone design effectively, drawing upon the eight main existing vocabularies.

This new language and its supporting methodology will, in the course of time, evolve from these eight disparate sources into a coherent and dynamic system which will in turn produce a new set of icons. The nature of the world wide web and its global reach will therefore shape some of the criteria for a universally understood and hopefully well-designed visual language, not bland corporate homogeneity as personified by the existing visual language of the multinational corporations but a vibrant and distinctive visual language which constantly draws upon the varied regional cultures of this planet.

The distance which has still to be 'travelled' to arrive at this point is shown repeatedly in the numerous accidents which occur in the existing use of visual culture on a regular basis. For example, domestic appliances, which in the West appear in white, use a colour associated with mourning in the Middle East. Hand signs and facial gestures which appear harmless in one country can be highly insulting in another. Finally, words provide an endless source of potential pitfalls and amusement:

> *...Mitsubishi originally introduced its Montero vehicle as the Pajero. Unfortunately, pajero is Spanish for masturbator and the Latin American market scoffed. There's a famous perfume called CoCo on the market. Coco is Portuguese slang for faeces...*[4]

To employ all eight methodological vocabularies without consistent research in a global market is at best irresponsible.

One final element needs to be thrown into the multimedial melting pot, that of the question of copyright in this digital age. Digital copyright has become an exceptionally complex minefield. With the lack of clear and precisely defined rules, the issue is seemingly as blurred as any of the effects available in any of the many software packages such as Photoshop or Photopaint.

Given the global scale of the web, the ability to borrow and digitally alter not just coding, but layouts, typefaces, text and images (and never seek permission), cite sources or indeed negotiate contracts, is a massive problem. Just when does someone else's image, which has been scanned in and then digitally manipulated, cease to be theirs?

Of equal concern is the race by large organisations to own digital copyright of images, famous/national collections, etc. If this is taken to the extreme, how long will it be before everyday objects and buildings in the public domain become subject to successful copyright claims?

As a subject it is seemingly overlooked and just not mentioned in most of the numerous books now available on web and multimedia design. Tay Vaughan's *Multimedia Making it Work* (4th edn) is a refreshing exception to this rule. It is essential therefore that students and designers are aware of these issues and maintain a good up-to-date knowledge of the changes to the laws of digital copyright.

What does all this mean for designers? Well, certainly the impact that all of this change is offering will allow for a re-run of the 1984 DTP revolution but on a far larger scale and far more quickly. The DTP revolution destroyed in quick time (no pun intended) whole sections of the traditional graphic design and allied print industry. Equally, the quality of much that was initially produced was questionable, to put it mildly. Mystique and tradition were ruthlessly swept away. Suddenly anyone who could use a keyboard and had access to a computer could be a designer. Well now a second revolution, barely 15 years after the first had dismantled much of what had taken 450 years to develop, is engulfing a much larger audience and this time dismantling barriers between different forms of communications, some of which themselves have only been in existence for a century at best.

In many ways this revolution has parallels with the arrival of cheap mass production methods of printing in the 1960s, when photocopiers and cheap offset printing allowed all sorts of people and organisations previously undreamed of opportunities to go into print. The underground press, with such famous magazines as *Oz*, *IT* and *Black Dwarf* all challenged the previously sacred tenets of design, press control, censorship, pornography, copyright, etc. Just over three decades later these same issues are raising their heads yet again in relation to the Web.

A short time spent surfing the net reveals so much which ranges from the bizarre to the banal, weird and occasionally breathtaking. Why are there so many sites devoted to every conceivable (or otherwise) aspect of and use for hamsters? Why should anyone wish to visit, more than once, a site devoted to watching paint peel? (www.amused.com/paintcam) or learn about ferrets in the history of art (http://web0.tiac.net/users/drbeer/joyce/ferrets/frhistpg.htm). The more obscure, it would seem, the better. Take, for instance, interest groups like the pencil sharpener club of Holland (www.xs4all.nl/ffigdlk/index.html). The list is endless but all of this has been designed and the web and number of web users are increasing exponentially.

In 1996 Neville Brody wrote that:

> ...*Electronic publishing provides a vital network for individualised communication of being able to publish ideas and thoughts that would not normally be given the time of day on any major network or in any major publication. It reverses the trend of mass media, splintering monosyllabic multinational chunks of information into personalised and humanistic messages...The events of the next two years will be critical – it is during this period that both the textual and visual rules of the media will be established...*[2]

Four years on it is clear that no such textual and visual rules have yet been established. The pace of technological development is unrelenting, allowing ever more opportunities to an ever widening group of people.

What is clear is that students will not only need to possess the essential pre-requisite of curiosity but also to have an ability to manipulate information in a wide range of non-linear ways – in short, to be able to create a range of visual narratives.

I would leave the final words on the subject to a prophetic quotation from Emil Ruder, a man whose seminal book *Typography* did more to encapsulate and popularise the International or Swiss Graphic style and in doing so lay the foundations for so much of the appearance of late 20th century print-based design.

> *Modern man thinks in contrasts. For him surface and space, far and near, inner and outer are no longer incompatible for him there is not only an 'either or' but also a 'both and'...*[6]

101   **References**

1   Birkerts, Sven. *The Gutenberg Elegies – The fate of reading in an electronic age*. London: Faber & Faber 1996, p.153

2   Brody, Neville. in Velthoven, William and Seijdel, Jornde, *Multimedia Graphics*. London: Thames & Hudson, London 1996, p.10–11

3   Chartier, Roger. *The Culture of print: Power and the uses of print in early modern Europe*. Cambridge: Polity Press, 1989, p. 2

4   Fernandes, Tony. *Global interface design.*London Academic Press Ltd,1995, p.118

5   Ochsenreiter, G. in Vaughan, T. *Multimedia making it work* (4th Ed.) Berkley, California Osborne/McGraw-Hill, 1998, p.5

6   Ruder, E. *Typography*. Zurich, Arthur Niggli, 1971

7   Veen, Jeffrey *Hot wired style – principles for building smart web sites*. San Francisco, Wired Books Inc, 1997 p.61

8   ibid. p.88

9   ibid. p.137

Mirjam Southwell worked for Voluntary Service Overseas (VSO) in Sudan for two years as a designer and marketing advisor with Ethiopian refugees after studying industrial design in the UK. On her return she went to the Royal College of Art to study product design, gaining an MDes (RCA). She has since worked as a designer, as lecturer in design and as a consultant evaluating development projects. During this time she completed an MSc in Comparative Development and International Policy at the University of Bristol and followed this with a PhD in the international policy process for technology, design, women and development. She continues to research in the areas of design and development, gender and technology.

The chapter looks both at the way in which designers perceive development and development perceives design. The development talked about is the attempt by countries in the North to develop the world's under developed or developing countries in the South. The focus is on product design but clearly many of the issues are relevant to all design practice.

The chapter uses terms that are problematical and the first major dilemma is whether or not to use the term 'Third World' to describe the group of countries where development is an issue. The "Third World" is probably the term we most recognise and use when talking about developing countries. However, there has been increasing unease with this term because of a raised awareness of its potential racism and colonial overtones and also because it no longer accurately describes a number of East Asian countries included when the term was originally coined in the 1950s.[4] The term 'Third World' offers a 'dubious homogeneity' Berger suggests, and we should not look for a new term but forget labels altogether. This has proved to be an impossible task in the context of this chapter and the label 'South' is used where a collective term is necessary. Similarly, the label 'North' is used where a collective term is needed to describe Europe, America, etc.

What development is

In the context of this chapter development is the word we use in the North to describe the work we do in the South. To explain development briefly, there have been and continue to be many development theories, for example dependency; modes of production; neo-liberalism; modernisation, etc. However, despite these and other theories, development continues to fail as much of what we see on the television and read in the newspapers shows. Large numbers of the world's population continue to live in appalling poverty, deprived of even the most basic needs – clean water, sufficient food, adequate shelter. Why the continued failure has been and continues to be is the subject of much debate. Blaming 'internal' factors such as a country's climate and culture, political and bureaucratic ineptitude, etc. and then imposing modernising solutions has been unsuccessful (Chew & Denmark[11], also see Frank[23] and Ingham[34]). There is the argument that development has simply become a drive for global consumerism and that the theories reflect this in their emphasis on economic determinants, particularly modernisation theory (Stewart[59] Chowdry[14] Hirshman[33]).

Development issues are complex, so not surprisingly the literature defining and explaining it is vast. Development is indeed 'a most elusive concept'[16]. That development is multi-dimensional, necessarily requiring the 'reorganization and reorientation of entire economic and social systems'[62] might be acknowledged but is rarely acted on in practice where the emphasis continues to be put on modernist assumptions, the rational ideal of the global market.[22] Development exists within the capitalist world-system where there are producers and non-producers and the driving force is global accumulation.[45]

'Alternative' development theories

There are 'alternative' development theories, including participation and empowerment. These are intended to be 'bottom-up' approaches to development where the people being 'developed' drive the agenda. However, as Brohman[9] asserts, for true 'bottom-up' development there has to be fundamental change in the global status quo and this is where alternative theories get difficult to address. Development, as Scott[13] argues, continues to be defined implicitly as markets, nations and productivity and this implicit definition links design to development. The South Commission[56], a group of experts from developing countries, argues that true development has not only to be people-centred but must achieve what people themselves see to be their social and economic interests.

Essentially, the word development conveys well-intentioned motives but as Pearce et al[49] point out since 'development' is a value word, implying change that is desirable, there is no consensus as to its meaning. It is important to remember this when considering design for development. Our perceptions, in the North, of what it is like in the South have been built on over two hundred years of 'Western-centric' history[31] and inevitably the cultural perceptions of need are tremendously strong. So the term 'development' is not to be used lightly; it should be used to indicate empowerment not control; mutual respect not superiority.

Designers view of development

The area of design for development and design in developing countries is highlighted by the relative absence of attention paid to these issues by design theorists and practitioners commenting on their practice. An example of this can be found in the first Humane Village journal published in 1994 by the Humane Village Centre for Compassionate Design in collaboration with the International Council of Societies of Industrial Design (ICSID). Arguably this is one publication from the design profession that should tackle the issues raised by development. There are comments on establishing a 'more closely detailed landscape of intimate, humane, values'.[42] Similarly to the 'alternative' development theory discourse, Childers[12] argues that there has been a global ideological drive towards the 'false perception that poverty is going to be defeated by "the magic of the Market"'. Regrettably however, the text has only two tentative mentions of developing countries.

In the North perceptions of design for development continue to be influenced by texts first published nearly three decades ago (for example see Papanek,[48] and Schumacher[54]). Much of what was written still holds true; however, the recognition that all people, regardless of how and where they live, want the 'best' is smothered under a blanker of moralising and nostalgia. More recently Whiteley[69] has reintroduced the concept of the 'socially responsible' designer but this is restricted to issues such as designing pedal-powered washing machines for Brazilian shanty towns. Arguably such a washing machine could have considerable kudos if featured in a lifestyle magazine as the 'green' exercise machine. Experience of working with people forced to live in the most dire of circumstances in Sudan illustrated for me Dormer's[17] assertion that there are objects 'that we want around us to lend colour, variety or expression to life'. This is no less true if you live in a mud hut with a flour sack for a roof in the middle of a refugee camp.

Design practice

As private businesses, design consultancies have to make money; obviously this influences the design projects they undertake. Designing for development is seen as a good cause rather than a money-maker. It is undertaken to counter the cynicism of designing for capitalist, developed consumerism which is the main source of employment for consultancies. The rationale for doing any design for development is tied to the emotional response of wanting to make a difference to people's lives. Designers use development to escape consumerism whilst the dominating development theories and practice emphasise the need for economic modernisation and market developments (at global and local levels – there is extensive literature covering this: see Scott[55] Chowdry[14] Hirshman[33] for review and critique). There is an ambivalence expressed towards undertaking design for development. It is morally right but commercially risky yet design is essentially about people.

Design consultancies may undertake the design of a product aimed at developing countries because they welcome the opportunity to do something that they perceive to be outside the consumer market, with a different objective, a chance to really improve lives. Integrity is one different objective where this is associated with the product for developing countries being a piece of 'appropriate technology', reflecting the work of Papanek[48] and Schumacher.[54] Design for developing countries is designing for the 'real world' and consequently basic and cheap products (cheap aesthetics as well as price) are needed. Products need to have integrity and to not look like a Western consumer product. Products for development are often thought to lose integrity when the aesthetics reflect Western consumerism as opposed to 'string and bamboo' appropriate technology, challenging the romanticism of the 'bush'. Design for development cannot be carried out in the capitalist market structure.

There are few examples of products aimed at developing countries being successful in the North. The Bayliss clockwork radio is one notable exception. Arguably designers fail to see a product's potential because they get caught up emotionally in their imagined reality of designing for development. This might point to a typical feeling when designing for developing countries, one of being charitable. The emotional needs of designers are being responded to, not the users' physical needs.[67] There is a demand for consumer goods in developing countries, as Ranis[52] points out; involving these consumers in the design process could go some way to satisfying basic needs. Design for capitalist consumerism might lead to a consultancy's success but it fails to address the romanticised 'other's' needs. Unlike designing for capitalist consumerism, it is apparently necessary to have both a global and political conscience to undertake design for development, to become a socially responsible designer.[69]

Perhaps because being successful is equated with financial profit and designing for development is associated with charity, undertaking design for development lacks credibility and is associated with 'the alternative' and being unprofessional. Being very successful and high profile might ensure a designer is not ridiculed by the profession but there is still too high a risk that this will happen. Design is exclusive rather than inclusive, a masculine approach tied up with ownership and control. Design has become an 'expert' profession which is able to be both exclusive (predominantly white, male and from the North), yet at the same time claim inclusivity through designing products for people. Designers' notions of what developing countries should access regarding products are influenced by romantic visions of the bush; Western aesthetics and expensive looking products are not appropriate. This points to the North's control of aesthetics at a global level – from mass produced consumer durables to handicrafts. Design consultancies' perceptions of developing countries based on the 'Third World bush' is not dissimilar from many development projects. Although the 'other' is identified as a producer, implicit imperialism dominates and the 'other' becomes a passive recipient of aid. The concept that products designed in the North for developing countries need to have integrity refers to a number of things: charitable honesty on the part of the designer, form very clearly following the product's function and a product which will not become a superficial consumer durable. Paradoxically, design from developing countries, visualised in handicrafts, has in many instances become dishonest and lost its cultural integrity. This is because it has to be adaptable to markets in the North and meet these so-called needs (this is discussed in more detail later). It too has to be functional but this is what the consumer wants; in developing countries the consumer is rarely asked what she or he might want.

Design offers 'status and rewards' to designers but rarely encourages part-icipatory design; designers rarely have to seriously consider 'others' (Goodall[28] Walsh et al[67]). This has profound consequences for designing for development and will ultimately fail to provide products that the users need and want. Yuval-Davis's[71] concept of 'universalist racism' which 'inferiorizes others as un-modern' is illustrated frequently by design for development.

Developments' view of design

Design theory and literature as designers' know them are largely inaccessible to development practitioners and design is rarely mentioned or discussed as having a role in development. The perception of what and who designers are, even if this is unconscious, does influence the way design is considered in development projects, or rather not considered. This happens even when development practitioners have themselves experienced the benefits of design. For example, producers painting 'go faster stripes' on oil presses in Sudan sell more than their competitors. Producers in developing countries do consider aesthetics as another example illustrates – painting the handles of agricultural tools black to differentiate the product in the market place. Development professionals may admire the initiative of the producer but there is still a prevailing belief that this is cheating in some way. Development practitioners fail to understand that design is more that a 'promotional veneer'.[39]

The lack of entrepreneurial trade is one cause of under development[32] and design is an essential component in addressing this. The right products, Zoomers[72] observes, not necessarily the right technology will help small and medium enterprises develop. Design clearly has a role to play here and although many development organisations' projects aim to develop small and medium size manufacturing enterprises (SMEs), they are invariably unaware of design or have a limited understanding of what it can offer. For example, products can be manufactured in Africa as consumer durables with potential global markets. Design can and should have a central role, linking manufacturing with the markets. Products can be designed that are manufacturable with simple techniques and that appeal to the market at the same time. However, in development organisations' product design often just gets done. If it is thought about at all, product design may be seen as a covert activity to be kept in the closet because of its association with art. An explanation for this lack of design awareness is that up until very recently, development organisations were rarely involved in the production of explicit consumer products (other than craft). An aspect of this is the emphasis development organisations have placed on the engineering design of what is called 'appropriate technology'. The term 'appropriate technology' conjures up images of string and bamboo constructions and not surprisingly these have not been considered consumer products.

There is limited recognition that product design can be beneficial to manufacturing and light engineering in both formal and informal sectors. Formal design is largely invisible in the product development process although consumers in developing countries are clearly influenced by a product's design, at least at a subconscious level. They may be regarded as conservative in their decision-making about what products to buy. Not having much money to spend is clearly going to influence choice. People are wary of the unknown and are reluctant to take risks, so involving the consumer in the design of possibly more efficient versions of a product may be a way to address this. Asking for feedback at the end of the process is not the most efficient use of limited time and resources.

Lamont[38] suggests that 'designing in Africa is very different to designing in other parts of the world', requiring careful study and observation of markets. Quite why it is so different is not explained: any product designing, to be successful, requires study and observation of the markets. One difference may be that the role and relevance of design is not obvious to manufacturing companies and enterprises in developing countries (although this is also a frequent criticism made of UK manufacturers by UK designers). The use of design in development can increase the dependency on external markets (Lyon[40]) by not responding to the need for domestic mass consumption markets before export for sustainable development.[41] Two perspectives are presented by consultants working for a recent development project managed in Europe and implemented in Africa. Adjasoo[1] argues that the export of traditional products is, 'the only way out for the resuscitation of the economy'; Wienholt[70] suggests that the success of handicraft production 'could help form the basis for the creative development of African industrial products because of their specifically African sense of form and design'. Design is used in development, at least implicitly in projects that promote craft production for economic development. The general tenor of these projects reflects Renne's[53] argument that the inter-relation between the trad-itional and the modern is obscured in handicraft as promoted for development and that this reinforces its association with economic marginality.

The World Bank published two reports that both mention design. The Bank's 1995 report focuses on three African countries; Ghana, Kenya and Zimbabwe and states that 'advanced product design skills are not in evidence among the firms in the three countries' nor do technical support institutions 'offer assistance in design'.[6] Some degree of designing does take place through copying or modifying local or foreign products. Modifications are made by firms in order to 'make use of local raw materials, to suit local tastes and to differentiate their products from rivals'. The report suggests that an expected outcome of trade liberalisation and foreign competition was a 'significant introduction of new products and product designs' but this has not happened. Claims of new products are in fact just adaptations of already existing artefacts. The report asserts that the 'ability to produce according to own design is an important measure of a firm's technological capabilities'. The report is negative in its response to attempts made by manufacturing firms to design products; for example, it says that in Zimbabwe 'fundamental design was not a widespread skill'. The report is also dismissive of adapting and copying particularly when the intention is to meet local markets' demands. This negative approach to adaptation and copying reveals a lack of understanding of the product design process. Completely new products happen relatively rarely and are usually as the result of new technological developments, for example the Sony Walkman and Dyson vacuum cleaner (and materials, e.g. carbon fibre, and production processes). Everyday product design largely consists of adaptation, refinement, 'tweaking' and often copying existing designs. The product's aesthetics, materials and manufacturing process (any one or combination), can be altered to present a new product to the market. Products are always undergoing change to meet the demands (real or assumed) of the local market, for example the Braun toaster in black sold well in Germany but was thought to be unsaleable in the UK until relatively recently.

In Zimbabwe the report found that at least '80 percent of the firms surveyed introduced some changes to a product's design'.[6] Clearly this finding can be taken as a positive indication of initiative and creativity present in the firms. A positive response to the abilities shown for even minor adaptations indicates the potential for design training and the need for design policy (see Ghose[26] and Pido[50]). Product design is identified as being 'crucially important for ethnic products', European consumers expecting 'authentic product design plus functionality'.[7] Skills and creativity of ordinary people are, suggests Cooley,[15] society's most precious assets. The reports offer an important indication that design is being recognised as having an integral role in development. However, although design is clearly visible in both reports, what is not visible is how design skills are to be developed and enhanced.[58] This issue is highlighted in four UNIDO (United Nations Industrial Development Organisation) studies looking at women's production enterprises in four developing countries. In craft enterprises it was found that new product designs sold for a higher price than traditional artefacts; all four studies comment on women's inadequate design skills but fail to offer ideas on how this is to be addressed.[64]

Design perceived by developing countries

There is, of course, a third perspective that is not highlighted in the chapter's title. Those being 'developed' at the receiving end of development also have a perspective on both design and development. Writers from developing countries, Ghose[26] and Pido[50], acknowledge design as both an ancient activity and an activity of everyday life (see also Gabor[24]). Ghose[26] argues that the governments of developing countries have to 'introduce national design policies that will dovetail with developmental policies, thereby making design an agent of the visual manifestation of the ideologies of development'. Acknowledging that there is a need to fit indigenous design to the cash economy, Pido[50] suggests that design could be used to combine skilled hand production and the national economic interest to 'produce consumer goods for ourselves'. But an absence of indigenous design capability 'makes it easier for hegemonic cultural projects to become naturalised'.[71] Clearly we cannot and must not assume that we know what this 'third' perspective is. What we can do is ask ourselves where we see design from developing countries. Design from developing countries is usually presented to us in the form of handicrafts. We probably do not actually think of craft artefacts from developing countries as having been designed and almost certainly do not consider them to be consumer durables. Crafts are made by hand, from natural materials with no moving parts (electronics, 'chips' etc.). Development organisations work to promote this perception; for example, Traidcraft and Oxfam both use photographs of craft producers using their hands and limited technology in their advertising.[57]

Who does the designing and where is also an issue; development projects want typical ethnic designs but it is invariably designers from the North doing the designing. The previously mentioned development project managed from Europe and implemented in Africa strives for traditional Africa design within the restrictions of European trends. This indicates the trap of cultural imperialism disguised as design for development. The identity of the designer and their relative power position influence aesthetics and value placed on the artefact. Astoury[2] illustrates, perhaps unwittingly, the paradox that the design of handicrafts finds itself in. He first says that 'On contact with the powerful economy of the western world the delicate economy based on craftsmanship which was indigenous to Africa...were literally cannibalized' and later argues that the craft sector 'represents a true economic potential [which can] increase [the] repute of the country as an export country'. A number of individuals involved in the project and writing in a 1997 publication refer to need for ethnic yet fashionable products, designed to meet the lifestyle needs of the European consumer (e.g. see Thiam[60] Mthing[47] Eiligmann[20] Pirie[51]). Astoury[2] argues that products designed by European designers 'must be a recognisable mirror of African identity of our day'. These comments highlight the paradox and difficulty of trying to rationalise westernised design and traditionalised craft. The producers of 'ethnic' African craft are responding to the North's perceptions of what is African. The global market is eroding cultural difference and what is left of cultural difference is packaged and labelled as ethnic and traditional (Turner[63] du Gay et al[25]). Despite the recognition that objects have meanings[37], artefacts are 'traditionalised' for the European markets by designers where consumers want authenticity but expect functionality too.[6] Contemporary African craft and design is not what is being promoted. African design and designers are being controlled by the European market and this restricts development through limiting innovation and creativity.[21]

Cultural imperialism is still very evident; developing countries continue to be controlled through their traditional artefacts. Ethnic origin must be tangible but not pre-dominate, says van Eeckhout;[19] 'every object must radiate genuiness and simplicity'. Dependency continues through the emphasis on design and production to meet the so-called needs of the North and romanticised perceptions of the historically 'simple' African, Asian or 'other'. There is also the double whammy of the supposed global market. For example, the North does not want anything too African but seeks a westernised tradition. African producers have to get to grips with the differences between countries, although the project supposedly reflects the unified European market which has replaced national ones.[29] A 'Western veneer' is placed over African reality and indigenous products.[46] Arguably trans-national companies are influencing cultural taste on a global scale[35] and design clearly plays a key roles in this phenomenon. The trans-global product is seen as a positive thing, part of an international language, although indigenous culture has also to be preserved. The other can be manipulated through visual culture (Childs and Williams[13] Chowdry[14]). Consequently, the preservation of a developing country's culture is at the mercy of the trans-national companies and international design, as are gender constructions[5]. Attempts by indigenous designers and writers about design to influence national design through practice and policy (see Pido[50] Ghose[26]), are stymied by global capitalist structures.

A gender perspective

As designers we impose a cultural, ethnic homogeneity on the South. We impose a similar homogeneity on the people living in the South. Of particular importance for design for development is gender difference. We may see starving or homeless or poor people but within this are the extremes of gender bias which, as Durning[18] notes are the 'primary cause of poverty'. Most importantly, he goes on to say that a sustainable economy is impossible because of these extremes of gender bias evident in many countries (not only the developing ones). Gender issues need consideration by product designers undertaking development projects, not least because as a profession it continues to be overtly male dominated. If designs are undertaken from the premise of gender neutrality or assumed knowledge of gender difference, the extremes of gender bias become further entrenched. Women's realities are rendered invisible. Introducing new technologies and designs can greatly strengthen the male's position in the household to the detriment of the female. Men invariably take over responsibility for women's tasks when the tasks are mechanised.[66] An example of a seemingly gender neutral project is that of a solar powered lamp being introduced in Southern Africa. Market research identified different male and female 'needs' for the lamp: men want the lamp to listen to the radio by in the evening, women to help their children do their homework. A seemingly non-problematical difference; however, men may have more purchasing or 'traditional' power within the household. The lamp may be used to meet his entertainment need before the educational needs of his children – is this a sound development objective? Another example could be the design of a motor scooter. Looking at the gender issues of individual transportation may lead one to ask questions of women's needs in communities where they have limited freedom to travel outside the confines of their home. As Attfield[3] says, design has the power to generate and reproduce patterns of dominance through objects and representations – the designer reinforces the invisibility of women. This refers to design in the North but it also has clear implications for design and development.

Importantly, women have to be seen as producers and active participants in global economics. Women are more than passive reproducers (see Waring[68] and Gibson-Graham[27]). In fact, in developing countries the majority of small enterprises are owned and operated by women. Mead and Liedholm[44] also note that because these enterprises tend to be home based, the women become 'invisible entrepreneurs'. Women are involved in food processing, textiles, craft production and also in the more unexpected areas of building, metal and wood work. However, their design requirements and design skills are invariably overlooked, simply not seen by development practitioners and designers alike. Women are rarely thought of as consumers, although Moss[46] suggests that women are essential to African self-sufficiency and could be used to create a 'new consumer society'.

Conclusions

In development there is a general lack of understanding or awareness of what product design actually is, relating to perceptions of design as art and only to do with aesthetics, not technology. The lack of good product designs and inadequate design skills is noted by some development organisations' publications but at no point do they comment on how this could be addressed. The impression is that design is simply supposed to happen as a natural phenomenon. Design practice is essentially invisible in development – designers are the experts, remaining detached from the user. There is still a reluctance to consider the aesthetics of technology. Indeed, there is an unease with the area of aesthetics and this is where design is associated. Design may be referred to as a trick and associated with weirdoes, ex-hippies, divergent thinking, things not of the mainstream. This may illustrate a more universal belief about design, that it is not concerned with the nitty gritty real world. From the development perspective, the emphasis on manufacturing for export denies the importance of the local market for development. It also denies the importance of artefacts to cultural identity, placing the emphasis on either 'pseudo-tradition' or globalised consumer products (perhaps these are becoming one and the same thing – Coca Cola and carved wooden giraffes available everywhere). Assuming that people will continue to want products that they do not really need (who decides that?), might provide a starting point for assessing what to design and how: If we have 'designer' water filters in the North, why not designer water filters in the South?

For designers in the North there clearly are differences between designing for small manufacturing enterprises in developing countries and designing for industrialised, often international companies. However, we can see that the similarities outweigh the differences. Considerations of quality, aesthetics, performance and cost of a product apply equally in development and developed contexts where people have a desire to use products[10] and need products regardless of ethnicity, class and gender. There is the suggestion that insufficient emphasis is placed on product design because of a preoccupation with the 'ceaseless creation of new technologies'.[36] In development the technologies may not be 'new' but there is undoubtedly a preoccupation with technology and, as the literature indicates, little emphasis on design, an exception being Wad[65] who briefly raises product design and development as a technology policy issue. Understanding the role of design is critical to understanding its importance for development; as Dormer[17] asserts, the role of designers is to package technology to make it accessible, desirable and useable (also see Bonsiepe.[8]) Therefore design is the interface between technology and people and consequently is in some part responsible for the creation of identities and influencing cultural change[57]. As technology cannot be discourse free[30], designers have considerable responsibility although Walsh et al[67] maintain that products are often designed more for the needs of the designer than the user. du Gay et al[25] suggest that designers can be 'defined as people involved in the provision of symbolic goods'.

Designing for development does, however, raise complex issues. This is not to suggest that projects should not be undertaken but, and it is a big but, the designer needs to understand the wider project environment. For development to be successful a detailed evaluation at a grassroots level is necessary. The same detailed evaluation of the needs of the user is essential before any design for a 'development' product ventures off the drawing board. Participatory research has been considered by design theorists but 'naked egotism and brazen ambition' has won the day to date[69] with regard to design practice. The lack of women product designers, Walsh et al[67] suggest, leads to the application of women's tacit knowledge about women users' needs happening very rarely.

Similarly there are very few designers with 'diverse ethnic backgrounds'.[43] The focus of designing itself has to change argues Thomas-Mitchell[61] the process having to begin with an 'explicit consideration of user activities and perceptions'. There are obvious problems with this for designers interested in undertaking products for developing countries – ethnicity, gender, location, etc. are all potential stumbling blocks. The most important issue however, that has to be challenged is that of perception. Our perception of what it is to be developed and what it means to be under developed needs challenging. Design practice needs to come out of its cosy studio and take on the task of opening eyes.

References

1   Adjasoo, K. 'Exporting from Ghana – My experience'. *Arts & Crafts, EACH News*, Protrade/GTZ GmbH, Germany, 1997, p.29–30

2   Astoury, J-F. 'Importance and potential of African art and craftwork'. *Arts & Crafts, EACH News*, Protrade/ GTZ GmbH, Germany, March, 1997, p.37–41

3   Attfield, J. 'FORM/female FOLLOWS FUNCTION/male: Feminist critiques of design', in J. Walker (Ed.) *Design history and the history of design*.USA Pluto Press. 1989

4   Berger, M. 'The end of the "Third World"?' *Third World Quarterly, Journal Emerging Areas*, 15(2), 1994, p.257-75

5   Bernal, V. 'Islam, transnational culture, and modernity in rural Sudan', in M. Grosz-Ngate and O. H. Kokole (Eds) *Gender encounters: challenging cultural boundaries and social hierarchies in Africa*. New York and London, Routledge, 1997

6   Biggs, T., Shah, M., and Srivastava, P. (1995) *Technological capabilities and learning in African enterprises*, World Bank Technical Paper 288, Africa Technical Department Series, The World Bank, Washington, D.C. 1995

7   Biggs, T., Miller, M., Otto, C. & Tyler, G. *Africa can compete! Export opportunities and challenges for garments and home products in the European market*. World Bank Discussion Papers 300. Africa Technical Department Series. The World Bank, Washington D.C. 1996

8   Bonsiepe, G. 'The chain of innovation: Science, technology, design'. *Design Issues*, 11, 3 1995, p.33–6

9   Brohman, J. *Popular development: Rethinking the theory and practice of development*. Blackwell, Oxford & Massachusetts: Blackwell 1996

10   Buchanan, R. 'Wicked problems in design thinking', in V. Margolin & R. Buchanan (Ed.), *The idea of design: A Design Issues Reader*. USA & UK: MIT Press, 1995

11   Chew, S. C. and Denemark, R. A. (Eds) 'On development and underdevelopment' in *The underdevelopment of development: Essays in honour of Andre Gunder Frank*. Thousand Oaks, London, New Delhi: Sage 1996

12   Childers, E. 'Advance or decline?' in *Dialogue. The Humane Village Journal*, 1, 1, 1994, p.36–7

13   Childs, P. and Williams, P. *An introduction to post-colonial theory*. London & New York: Prentice Hall & Harvester Wheatsheaf 1997

14   Chowdry, G. 'Endgendering development? Women in development(WID) in international development regimes', in M. Marchand and J. Parpart (Ed.) *Feminism, postmodernism, development.* London & New York: Routledge 1995

15   Cooley, M. 'Socially Useful Design', in R. Roy & D. Wield (Eds) *Product Design & Technological Innovation: A Reader.* Milton Keynes: Open University 1986

16   Crush, J. (Ed.) *Power of development.* London & New York: Routledge, 1995

17   Dormer, P. *The Meanings of modern design: Towards the 21st century.* UK: Thames & Hudson, 1991

18   Durning, A. *Ending poverty.* World Watch Institute 1991

19   Eeckhout van, B. 'Paris – Maison & Objet? MIC '96'. *Arts & Crafts, EACH News,* Protrade / GTZ GmbH, Germany, March, 1997, p.80–2

20   Eiligmann, A 'Ouagadougou - International Fair for African handicraft / SIAO '96.' *Arts & Crafts, EACH News,* Protrade / GTZ GmbH, Germany, March, 1997, p.83–4

21   Fay, B. *Contemporary philosophy of social science: a multicultural approach.* Oxford: Blackwell, 1996

22   Ferguson, A. 'Bridge identity politics: An integrative feminist ethics of international development'. *Organization,* 3, 4, 1996, p.571–587

23   Frank, A. G. The underdevelopment of development, in S. C. Chew and R. A. Denemark (eds.)*The underdevelopment of development: Essays in honour of Andre Gunder Frank.* Thousand Oaks, London, New Delhi: Sage 1996

24   Gabor, D. 'Compulsive Innovation', in R. Roy & D. Wield (eds.) *Product Design & Technological Innovation: A Reader.* Milton Keynes: Open University 1986

25   Gay du P., Hall, S., Janes, L., Mackay, H. & Negus, K. *Doing cultural studies: The story of the Sony Walkman.* Milton Keynes: Open University and London: Sage, 1997

26   Ghose, R. 'Design, development, culture, and cultural legacies in Asia', in V. Margolin & R. Buchanan (Eds), *The idea of design: A Design Issues Reader,* MIT Press 1995

27   Gibson-Graham, J. K. *The end of capitalism (as we knew it): A feminist critique of political economy.* Oxford, Blackwell 1996

28   Goodall, P. Design and Gender. *Block,* 9, 54, 50-61 (1983)

29   Graf Hardenberg, A. Editorial. *Arts & Crafts, EACH News,* Protrade / GTZ GmbH, Germany, March, 1997, p.9

30   Grint, K. & Woolgar, S. 'On some failures of nerve in contructivist and feminist analyses of technology', in R.Gill and K.Grint (eds.), *The gender – technology relation: contemporary theory and research.* UK & USA: Taylor & Francis 1995

31   Groot de. J. 'Conceptions and misconceptions: The historical and cultural context of discussion on women and development', in H. Afshar (ed.) *Women, development and survival in the Third World.* UK: Longman 1991

32   Himmelstrand, U. 'Perspectives, controversies & dilemmas in the study of African development', in U Himmelstrand, K. Kinyanui & E. Mburugu (eds.) *African perspectives on development: Controversies, dilemmas & openings.* London: James Currey, 1994

33 Hirshman, M. 'Women and development: A critique', in M Marchand & J Parpart (Eds) *Feminism, postmodernism, development*. London & New York: Routledge 1995

34 Ingham, B. *Economics and development*. London: McGraw-Hill 1995

35 Kaplinsky, R. 'The economies of small: Appropriate technology in a changing world'. *Intermediate Technology*, London 1990

36 Kennedy, J. *Papers in science technology and public policy*. The Technical Change Centre London 1985

37 Krippendorff, K. 'On the essential contexts of artifacts or the proposition that "design is making sense (of things)"', in V. Margolin & R. Buchanan (eds.). *The idea of design: A Design Issues Reader*, MIT Press 1995

38 Lamont, V. 'Designing in rural Kenya'. *Arts & Crafts, EACH News*, Protrade / GTZ GmbH, Germany, p.43 1997

39 Lorenz, C. 'Design Policy: A resurgence for UK Designers', in R. Roy and D. Wield (eds.) *Product Design & Technological Innovation: A Reader*. Milton Keynes: Open University 1986

40 Lyon, J. 'Money and power: Evaluating income generating projects for women', in N. Redcliff and M. T. Sinclair (eds.). *Working women: International perspectives on labour and gender ideology*. London & New York: Routledge 1991

41 Mamdani, M. A critical analysis of the IMF programme in Uganda, in U. Himmelstrand, K. Kinyanui and E. Mburugu (eds.) *African perspectives on development: Controversies, dilemmas & openings*. London: James Currey 1994

42 Manu, A. Minima Moralia. *The Humane Village Journal*, 1, 1, 13-15 1994

43 Martinez, G. 'How I see it / why diversity is good for design'. *Innovation, Journal of the Industrial Designers Society of America* 13, 2, 2-4 1994

44 Mead, D. and Liedholm, C. The dynamics of micro and small enterprises in developing countries. *World Development*, 26,1, 61-74 1998

45 Moghadam, V. *Gender and the development process in a changing global environment*. United Nataion University, World Institute for Development Economics Research 1993

46 Moss, B. A. 'To determine the scale of wants to the community': Gender and African consumption in, M. Grosz-Ngate & O. H. Kokole (eds.). *Gender encounters: challenging cultural boundaries and social hierarchies in Africa*. New York & London: Routledge 1997

47 Mthing, M. 'The project - an overview. *Arts & Crafts', EACH News*, Protrade / GTZ GmbH, Germany, March, 17-25 1997

48 Papanek, V. *Design for the real world: Human ecology and social change*. London: Thames & Hudson 1971/1985

49 Pearce, D., Barbier, E. and Markandya, A. *Sustainable development: Economics and environment in the Third World*. London: Earthscan 1990

50 Pido, O. 'Made in Africa'. *Design Review*, 4, 15, p.30–5 1995

51 Pirie, J. 'The handicraft market in Britain'. *Arts & Crafts, EACH News*, Protrade / GTZ GmbH, Germany, March, p.59–60 1997

52 Ranis, G. 'Appropriate technology and the development process', in F. Long and A Oleson (eds.). *Appropriate technology & social values: A critical appraisal.* Cambridge, Massachusetts: Ballinger 1980

53 Renne, E, P. 'Traditional Modernity and the economics of handwoven cloth production in Southwestern Nigeria'. *Economic Development & Cultural Change,* 45, 4, p.773–92 1997

54 Schumacher, E. F. *Small is beautiful: A study of economics as if people mattered.* London: Abacus, 1973/1987

55 Scott, C. V. *Gender and development: Rethinking modernization and dependency theory.* Boulder & London: Lynne Reiner 1995

56 South Commission. *The challenge to the South: The report of the South Commission.* Oxford: Oxford University Press 1990

57 Southwell, M. 'Magic by design: Technology transformed'. *Image & Text: Journal for Design,* 7, p.3–8 1997

58 Southwell, M. *Managing the invisible: Design for Third World development.* Paper presented at the Ninth International Forum on Design Management, New York, USA 1999

59 Stewart, F. 'Technology transfer for development', in R. Evenson & R.Ranis (eds.). *Science & technology: lessons for development policy.* Intermediate Technology, London 1990

60 Thiam, P. D. 'The challenges of globalized commercial promotion'. *Arts & Crafts, EACH News,* Protrade / GTZ GmbH, Germany, March, 13-17 1997

61 Thomas-Mitchell, C. 'Action, perception and the realization of design'. *Design Studies,* 16, p.4–28 1995

62 Todaro, M. *Economic development in the Third World.* London & New York: Longman 1993

63 Turner, B. S 'Actions, actors, systems', in the *Blackwell companion to social theory.* Oxford: Blackwell 1996

64 UNIDO. *Global industrial change: Women and socio-economic progress.* UNIDO, Vienna 1996

65 Wad, A. 'Science and technology policy', in J-J. Salomon, F. Sagasti and C. Sachs-Jeantet (eds.). *The incertain quest: Science, technology and development.* Tokyo, New York & Paris: UNU Press 1994

66 Wajcman, J. *Feminism confronts technology.* Cambridge: Polity Press 1993

67 Walsh, V., Roy, R., Bruce, M. and Potter, S. *Winning by design: technology, product design and international competiveness.* Oxford, Massachussetts: Blackwell 1992

68 Waring, M. *If women counted: A new feminist economics.* London: Macmillan 1989

69 Whiteley, N. *Design for society.* UK: Reaktion Books 1993

70 Wienholt, H. 'Africa – Partner for European trading'. *Arts & Crafts, EACH News,* Protrade/ GTZ GmbH, Germany, p.53–4 1997

71 Yuval-Davis, N. *Gender & Nation.* London, New Delhi: Sage 1997

72 Zoomers, E. B. 'Appropriate technology – is it right for small business?' *Small Enterprise Development* 4, 4, p.17–23 1993

globalisation

Stuart Durant

Stuart Durant studied architecture at the Architectural Association, failed to empathise with Brutalism – the prevailing architectural ideology of the time worked for a decade as a television designer and designed the first setting for satellite transmission – coincidentally an early manifestation of globalisation. While working in television he was invited to write an MA thesis at the Royal College of Art. Later he worked as an antiquarian bookseller, subsequently taught history of design and architecture – mainly at Kingston University where he became Reader and has published extensively on design and architecture. His writings have been translated into French, German, Japanese and Spanish. He has acted as consultant for several important exhibitions.

A 'life-changing phenomenon' – the internet – is speeding the development of universal awareness. But ideas have always crossed the frontiers of time and language without hindrance. Air travel and electronic communication have hastened what we have recently come to call 'globalisation'. In 1962 Marshall McLuhan coined the term 'global village'.[1] It instantly became part of everyday speech. A global village perfectly summed up what people had seen developing around them but had not been able to put into words. Globalisation is inevitable. People have always borrowed and imitated. Such is the nature of humanity. It is the rapidity of globalisation which we find disorienting. As I write this, new internet sites appear devoted to the concerns of globalisation. On the internet associations like the International Forum on Globalization (IFG) are preoccupied with the fact that the world's corporate and political leadership appears to be presiding over the restructuring of global politics and economics. My chapter will be out of date even before it is published.

Design is particularly susceptible to the process of globalisation. Five thousand years ago there were cultural exchanges between Mesapotamia and the civilization of the Indus valley. Long before the conception of nation existed ideas, shapes and patterns were borrowed and exchanged. The people of East Africa have been using pottery water coolers made in India for a thousand years. The Sioux invented the feathered headdress, the most potent emblem of the native American warrior. It was simply copied by the other tribes. Eastern designs have long been borrowed by the West. The ogee arch, with its double curves, was first used in Britain at the end of the 13th century. It was imported by the crusaders who had been impressed by Muslim buildings in the Holy Land. The ogee itself had originated in Buddhist India some nineteen hundred years before. Early Italian fabrics were often decorated with Arabic calligraphy or even with Chinese dragons.[2] In turn, the Chinese borrowed a Western technique – cloisonné enamelling, which had been developed in Byzantium.

The influence of a text is far easier to measure than anonymous techniques or designs. The oldest surviving architectural text is Vitruvius's *Ten Books of Architecture*.[3] Vitruvius's writings are the foundations upon which the whole elaborate edifice of post-medieval Western architecture and design – by default – was built. We will almost certainly never know who Vitruvius really was. All we know with certainty was that he was a Roman architect and military engineer who worked early in Augustus's reign. Manuscript copies of his treatise have been found in monastic libraries throughout Western Europe. The first printed version of his *De architectura. libri decem.* was published in Rome in about 1486. Editions soon appeared in all the major European languages. It was the first truly international treatise on the practical and aesthetic aspects of architecture. What is particularly instructive about the Vitruvius story is that he borrowed liberally from earlier Greek writers on architecture – notably Hermogenes, who had lived a century and a half earlier. In other words, Vitruvius's ideas were derived from foreign sources as well as from an earlier era.

Globalisation really began during the Enlightenment. *Diderot's Encyclopédie*, 1750-80 – one of the most glorious achievements of the 18th century – was postulated upon the notion that the entire world could be explained in rational scientific terms. The fact that much of the knowledge expounded in the 35 volumes of the *Encyclopédie* soon became hopelessly outmoded should not be allowed to obscure the work's profoundly radical nature. From hence onwards the world could – and increasingly would – be seen as a whole. In the spirit of the Enlightenment, William Jones, the greatest philologist of his age and the father of modern linguistics, jurist and orientalist, sympathetically interpreted Indian learning; Abbé J. A. Dubois wrote about Indian cosmology and manners; and Isaac Titsingh, of the Dutch East India Company, wrote about the culture of Japan.[4] The writings of these three scholars can be accounted among the first scientific studies of non Western cultures.

Globalisation gathered pace in the 19th century. Looking back on the preceding 50 years in 1887, Thomas Henry Huxley (1825-95), the great biologist and champion of Darwin, spoke of revolution – 'it is nothing less'. He wrote of : 'the wonderful increase of industrial production by the application of machinery... accompanied by an even more remarkable development of... locomotion and intercommunication' – which had created 'common interests among the most widely separated peoples'.[5] The interpenetration and interaction of different cultures was reflected in the literature of the era. Wilkie Collins's *Moonstone*, published in 1868, the best known of the Victorian sensation novels, deals with the theft and recovery of the diamond which adorned the forehead of the Hindu Moon God. After many vicissitudes, three pertinacious Brahmins, disguised as jugglers, manage to return the moonstone to India. Untypically for a Victorian, Collins does not question – and indeed appears to admire – the religious values of the Brahmins.

The most remarkable early description of burgeoning globality came in 1895 from the writer Max Nordau (1845-1922) – a Hungarian Jew who wrote in German.[6] With seven-league boots, Nordau presented what must be among the first descriptions of globalisation. He writes like a modern journalist.

The humblest village inhabitant has to-day a wider geographical horizon, more numerous and complex intellectual interests, than the prime minister of a petty, or even a second-rate state a century ago... he interests himself simultaneously in the issue of a revolution in Chile, in a bush-war in East Africa, a massacre in North China, a street row in Spain, and an international exhibition in North America

(The World Columbian Exhibition, Chicago 1893). A cook receives and sends more letters than a university professor did formerly, and a petty tradesman travels more and sees more countries and people than the reigning prince of other times.[7]

Just over a century ago we had already arrived at the point where people were beginning to recognise that we now lived in single indivisible world. The advance of technology – too often ignored as a determinant by the academic historian – was, as it is now, a principal factor in this progression. The secrets of the machine were learned quickly, though by no means painlessly. Once stable communities were often dismembered by industrialisation. We, however, are accustomed to impermanence and ephemerality.

By the 1830s, France, Germany and the United States of America were beginning to flex their muscles as industrial powers. Between 1840 and 1891 the length of rail track in Europe increased by a scarcely believable 72 times – to over two hundred thousand kilometres. During the same period the number of railway travellers had multiplied by 25 times. The number of letters received by the average citizen of Britain, France and Germany increased by more than four times. The numbers of newspapers – printed on steam powered printing presses – multiplied by almost six times. In Germany the number of books published increased by 17 times. The number of ships entering British ports between 1840 and 1890 increased almost eightfold. During the same period British merchant tonnage trebled. During the 50 years following 1840 world trade expanded more than two and a half times.[8]

Britain's position as the workshop of the world lasted barely a couple of decades. Soon, Austria and her satellites, as well as Russia, were developing their own manufacturing industries. By the 1870s, after less than 20 years' intercourse with the West, Japan had set up sizable textile industries. Heavy industries were soon to follow. In the last two decades of the 19th century enterprising Indian financiers imported British machinery and built modern textile plants – a matter of discomfort to the British authorities, who saw Britain's captive market for Lancashire cotton goods evaporating before their eyes.

The Great Exhibition of 1851 commemorated the triumph of industrialisation. Nearly six million people visited Paxton's Crystal Palace in Hyde Park – the greatest number of people who had ever congregated for a secular occasion.The Great Exhibition was the first international exhibition. Its full title was An Exhibition of the Works of Industry of All Nations. It was to be the first of 50 or so major international exhibitions.[9] Exhibits were sent by Australia, Austria, Belgium, Canada, France, Germany, Greece, Ireland, Italy, Malta, Russia, Spain, Sweden and Norway, Switzerland and the United States of America.

The arts of Algeria, China, India, Persia and Turkey, nations which had yet to industrialise, aroused great admiration. People marvelled, in particular, at the gorgeous textiles sent from India. These were analysed and dissected by authorities on design. Based on this study, quasi-scientific 'Principles' to regulate the colouring and designing of motifs were formulated by Owen Jones (1809-74). He was a polymath – architect, designer, orientalist, traveller, theorist and publisher. He is best known for his incomparable *Grammar of Ornament*, 1856 – the first global pattern book. Jones was the first to acknowledge that the various competing forms of historicism were irrelevant in a rapidly changing world and called for 'imaginative and intelligent eclecticism'. Under Jones's influence Indian motifs and colour schemes, evolved over the millennia, were quickly absorbed into the vocabulary of British designers. British machine-made textiles – once dowdy or coarse – were to surpass those of the other industrialised nations for several decades.

Thirty-eight years after the Great Exhibition came the greatest international exhibition of the century - the Paris Universal Exhibition of 1889.[10] Colossal changes had taken place since 1851. The steam age was over. Nine electric generating stations at the exhibition provided the power for the thousands of electric lamps which made day of the night. The modernity of the exhibits still astounds. There was opera in stereo by telephone, Edison's phonograph - which to the surprise of some could record speech in any language. The Eiffel Tower was the centrepiece of the exhibition; the arches at its base formed the triumphal entry. Electric searchlights at its summit illuminated distant farmhouses in the surrounding countryside. A dirigible flew above the Bois de Boulogne. Jets of spray from the battery of electrically illuminated fountains in front of the Palace of Industry changed colour in time to the music of brass bands. The immense Palace of Machines housed hundreds of working machines. Their deafening clatter created cross-rhythms of unimaginable complexity. This was the first steel building. It was built to exactly correspond with the height of Napoleon's column in the Place Vendôme. The great arches spanned 110 metres. Electric gantries, like the bridges of transatlantic liners, took visitors up and down its vast length. People could savour the future worlds of Jules Verne and H. G. Wells.

Visitors came from all over the world to the Champ de Mars and the Place des Invalides – 30 million of them. Six times as many as had gone to Hyde Park. There were national pavilions representing Bolivia, Britain, Holland, Japan, Mexico, Nicaragua, Persia, Rumania, Siam. In the colonial section there were complete villages – with their inhabitants – from Java, Oceania, Senegal. Douanier Rousseau discovered the exotic world here. Algerian musicians and dancers and a theatre from Indo-China entertained the public. The gamelan orchestra from the court of the Sultan of Solo so impressed Debussy that he began to experiment with the Javanese musical scale. Rodin drew the Sultan's dancers. Before the word had yet been invented, multiculturalism, of a kind – though not unmixed with condescension – had arrived upon the scene. Many of the visitors to the exhibition were French peasants. Their own villages – unchanged for generation upon generation – must have seemed almost as quaint to them as the plaster replica of a street from Cairo, adjacent to to the Palais des Machines. Working diligently in the picturesque winding street were its 60 inhabitants – jewellers, merchants, weavers. Peasants now knew that their own time-immemorial world would soon become history. The new age was everywhere about them.

Museums were founded to educate a public who were avid for information. They formed an integral part of the cultural life of the progressive 19th century city. The South Kensington Museum – renamed the Victoria and Albert Museum in 1899 – was opened in 1857.[11] In 1863 the Union Centrale des Beaux-Arts Appliqués à l'Industrie was founded in Paris, with South Kensington as the model. In 1864 Vienna set up a museum of the applied arts – the Kaiserliches Königliches Österreichisches Museum für Kunst und Industrie (Imperial Royal Austrian Museum for Art and Industry). It was very close to South Kensington in its organisation. Like the universal exhibitions, but without the accompanying sensationalism, such museums informed the public about artifacts from distant places and unfamiliar cultures.

The South Kensington Museum pioneered the collecting of the productions of the world beyond Europe. By the 1880s South Kensington had assembled collections from China, India, the Islamic countries and Japan. These were described in an admirable series of well-illustrated and inexpensive little books. These made previously unknown works of art and craft productions familiar to anyone who cared to study them.[12] Well-known textbooks for design students by authors like like A. H. Christie, Walter Crane, Lewis F. Day or Richard Glazier drew heavily upon the South Kensington collections for their information.[13]

Satiated as we are with television and latterly with internet images, it is impossible for us to feel the frisson of excitement which people once got from pictures of the exotic world. Distant places, where the rare and sometimes mysterious objects in the museums had been made, could be seen in photographs. Most of the images in the popular journals were in the form of engravings – initially on wood, later on steel. These steel-engravings were often copied by skilled technicians from photographs. This was particularly so with topographical images - like those which were published in such journals as *The Illustrated London News* or *le Monde Illustré* in Paris. In the late 1870s, with the advent of the photogravure method of reproduction, it became possible for photographic images to be reproduced easily and cheaply.[14] The photograph, though it lacked the spontaneity of the on-the-spot sketch, had an unassailable authenticity.

There were about 2500 photographers in Britain by 1860 – most, one can assume, supplying the familiar unsmiling, dark sepia, *carte-de-visite* portraits to the bourgeoisie. By the 1850s, the wet collodion process, though tedious by our standards, enabled photographers to set up their apparatus in remote places. The recording of the visual world could now begin in earnest. Roger Fenton photographed Russia and then the Crimean War of 1854–56. India and its people were documented by many fine photographers. Among them was Samuel Bourne who, with a troop of porters to carry his equipment, became the first photographer of the Himalayas. Then there were also R. B. Oakley – who photographed classical Hindu architecture in Southern India and W. W. Hooper - who recorded the devastating famine in Madras of 1876-78. India, which had captured imaginations in the 18th century, was knowable to everybody.

The Egypt of the Pharaohs was photographed by the journalist and novelist Maxime du Camp – the friend of Flaubert – and by Francis Frith; China by Captain R. Dew, B. F. K. Rives and J. Thompson – who recorded the self-same landscapes which one sees in the 8th century scroll paintings of Wang Wei. Among the most daring of the early global photographers was Felice Beato, a Venetian who became a British subject. He was noted for his records of devastation caused by military conflict. He photographed the physical damage of the Indian Mutiny of 1858 and the China War of 1860. Among his best known photographs, however, are of the alluring Japan of Hokusai's and Hiroshige's wood-block prints, which he took in the mid 1860s. Some were reproduced as steel engravings in Aimé Humbert's *Le Japon Illustré*, of 1870 – one of the earliest French accounts of contemporary Japan . Others appeared in *The Illustrated London News*.

125

People could buy for themselves cheap portrait photographs of any international celebrity who took their fancy. These stare unflinchingly at the brass and mahogany cameras, with their large lenses and their mysterious attendants concealed under black cloths. Their solemnly composed expressions are disquieting. But the precise definition of the photographs brings an ordinariness and a pathos to their faces. The craze for collecting cartes-de-visite of the famous was started by the Parisian photographer Disderi. Fame had become completely international. Photographic portraits circulated in their millions among middle-class collectors. Portraits abound of Hans Christian Andersen, Bismarck – who was presiding over the creating of modern Germany, Charles Dickens, the Archduke Ferdinand of Austria, Giuseppe Garibaldi – who was popularly credited with re-uniting Italy Victor Hugo – the greatest romantic writer of the century

President Abraham Lincoln, Franz Liszt – piano virtuoso and composer Ludwig II of Bavaria – who built the mad Wagnerian palace at Neuschwanstein Queen Victoria.[15] In 1882 Eadweard Muybridge toured Europe demonstrating his 'zoopraxiscope' by means of which consecutive still photographs of animals in motion could be projected onto a large screen. Here was the beginning of cinematography. Soon the cinema newsreel would be seen in every town. The world was shrinking.

The art magazine was a by-product of the industrial revolution. The international, and latterly global, character of these magazines is most striking. The prosperous urban middle class, expanding vastly in numbers, wanted to learn about art. Knowledge of art – and the possession of works of art – were important symbols of status, status which was still being fought for by these newcomers to polite society. The earliest of the British art magazines was *The Art Union* which was founded in 1839 by Samuel Carter Hall, a journalist who was married to a fashioUnable novelist. It started life as little more than a pamphlet. It was later re-named *The Art Journal* and survived until 1911. It was a handsome and sophisticated production which documented nearly all the major international exhibitions of the century in splendid detail. *L' Art pour Tous* – an 'encyclopaedia of industrial and decorative art' was founded in Paris in 1861. It was captioned in French, German and English - clearly for the burgeoning international readership.[16]

By far the most dynamic and influential of late 19th century art magazines was *The Studio*. This was published in London and first appeared in April 1893. It circulated throughout Europe and the United States. It was founded by the far-sighted Bradford entrepreneur Charles Holme and edited by the brilliant Gleeson White. There was a daring article on Aubrey Beardsley in the first issue. *The Studio* was abundantly illustrated with excellent photogravure reproductions of paintings, drawings, new architecture, furniture and textiles. From its inception it was completely international in tone. In its pages one sees the protean fin-de-siècle work of Peter Behrens, Carlo Bugatti, Georges de Feure, Eugène Grasset, Josef Hoffmann and the Wiener Werkstätte, Koloman Moser, Josef Maria Olbrich, Bernard Pankok, Richard Riemerschmid, Steinlen, Jan Toorop and Henry van de Velde. These are the first designer international mega-stars.

The Studio published, among its famous *Special Numbers*, handsomely-produced paperbacks on the folk arts of Austro-Hungary, Italy, Rumania and Russia. These contain some of the best colour reproductions of the era. Folk art became international property. Its delightful pre-industrial age idioms became part of the collective unconscious of a whole generation of designers in the decorative arts. From *The Studio*, in the pre-1914 years, Europeans learned of the doings of the Arts and Crafts Movement, then at its apogée. *The Studio's* international influence has yet to be fully measured. It will be proved to have been immense. The immensely successful *Studio* was widely emulated in Europe. A number of well-produced magazines, with a very similar format and contents, were started in the late 1890s. All were internationalist. They were *Art et Décoration*, Paris 1897; *Dekorative Kunst*, Munich 1897 and *Deutsche Kunst und Dekoration*, Darmstadt 1897. In 1898, from Vienna came *Ver Sacrum* – 'Sacred Spring' – the journal the Vienna Secessionists – which, though more literary in its contents, clearly shows its indebtedness to *The Studio*. Then, again in 1898, there came an elegant journal from Holland – *Bouw-en Sierkunst. Revue bimestrielle de l'art antique et moderne* which published in Dutch and French. *Mir Ikusstva*, a Russian art magazine – subtitled *Le Monde Artiste* - was published in 1899. It, too, was internationalist in its approach. Art, architecture and design were, beyond question, matters of global interest at the beginning of the 20th century.

Seventeen million people died in the First World War. Was it the destiny of Europe to culminate in the obscene butchery of the battlegrounds? At the Somme there were a million and a quarter casualties. A single pointless battle for dubious strategic ends. The Great War severed the arteries which had sustained Europe for more than a millennium. It damaged beyond repair the faith in an approachable and benign God. There was to be no consolation of faith for the succeeding generation. The war destroyed, too, the innocent and unquestioning faith in nation. And it made the once comforting and solemn rituals of the ruling dynasties seem preposterous. It seemed as if Europe had been betrayed by its own history. Our world was more uncomfortable now than it had ever been. A new and precarious age had arrived. J. B. Priestley described the war as 'a great jagged crack in the looking glass'.

A sense of 'yesterday' and 'tomorrow' pervaded the thinking of the post 1914-18 years. The gruesome war, it was widely said, had been the inevitable consequence of nations' vaingloriously harnessing the powerful forces of industry and capital for petty selfishly nationalistic ends. It had shattered the victors just as it had the vanquished. The new generation – who were to become the champions of the Modern Movement – tried to obliterate this past. They despised its academic arts, embodying, as they appeared to, the messages, the presumptions and the follies of old, quarrelsome, Europe, a Europe convinced of the divinely-ordained righteousness of its hierarchies.

The teachers at the Bauhaus, post-1918 Germany's experimental design academy, exhibited the current contempt for the lessons of history. Education at the Bauhaus begun with a blank slate – the *tabula rasa* – of simple 'creative' exercises. Of course, history cannot be expunged quite so easily. The exercises in the Preliminary Courses – *Vorlehre* – were, in the event, little more than extensions of the visual games of the teachers of pattern-making from before the war. The past is inescapable.

The Modern Movement was unequivocally international. Henry-Russell Hitchcock and Philip Johnson in their *The International Style. Architecture since 1922*, published in 1932, defined a mode which had come during the decade to dominate design and architecture throughout the world. It was to continue to do so for the next 30 years.The exponents of the style emphasised volume, with 'space enclosed by thin planes' - often walls of glass. They favoured 'regularity' – in place of conventional classical symmetry; and, for aesthetic effect, they depended upon 'the intrinsic elegance of materials... as opposed to applied ornament'. Hitchcock and Johnson illustrated work from all over Europe and the United States. They illustrated country houses, department stores, employment offices, exhibition buildings, factories, filling stations, flats, newspaper offices, old people's homes, schools, suburban houses. A yacht club, of 1931, by Joseph Emberton, at Burnham-on-Crouch on an estuary in Essex, could have been comfortably exchanged for Labayed's and Aizpurua's waterside club at San Sebastián in the Basque country. Soon the International Style had its adherents in Argentina, Brazil, India (a few), Mexico, South Africa. They had a moral passion for science and reason, sunlight and air, for informal, unhierarchical spaces in which rational dialogues could take place. They were impervious to the blandishments of nation and history.

The guardians of national traditions, the surviving advocates of the Arts and Crafts solution, seemed impossibly out of touch with the new age. They revered the rich accumulated skills and the collective imaginations of the generations which had gone before. They wished, vainly, to roll back the frontiers of technology. They hated the current 'mass-production spirit', as le Corbusier called it. The embattled rear guard of Ecole des Beaux Art dreaded the discarding of the classical dogmas which modernism would bring.

The CIAM – Congrès Internationaux d'Architecture Moderne – was founded in 1928 by Hélène de Mandrot, who was Swiss. CIAM was to be the first global architectural organisation. It met in different places – Frankfurt-am-Main, Brussels, the S.S. Patris – cruising in the Mediterranean sun between Marseilles and Athens, Paris. A well-intentioned left-wing paternalism prevailed at the CIAM congresses. Delegates unceasingly talked of the new architecture and the tower cities which were going to the transform the the lives of the masses.

In Germany, the Nazis were hostile towards internationalism. The Bauhaus had, by the late 1920s, gained an immense international reputation and had attracted students from all over the world. Skirmishes with the Nazis, who circulated grotesque tales of Bolshevist–Jewish conspiracies, brought about its closure in July 1933. The Nazis sought to revive a German style. This was no more than mawkish cinematographic make-believe. In their megalomania, the Nazis dreamed of overwhelming neo-classical structures – titanic monuments to the thousand-year Reich. To become noble ruins in the distant future. They ended as rubble.[17] Attitudes were different in Italy during the thirties. During the years of Mussolini's fascism the international-style was tolerated and, on occasions, even encouraged. Italian modernist architecture and design stands comparison with the best of the genre from Europe and America.[18] Mussolini's planned Rome World's Fair – 'E42' – was to have been triumphally and stylishly international-modern. It was summarily cancelled after the outbreak of the Second World War.

The Second World War was a re-run of the First. The wounds of 1914-18 had not healed. The tense and restless 1930s ended in the disaster which everyone had predicted. The right-wing and Fascist oligarchies – Germany, Italy and Japan were defeated in the end. The first atomic bomb was dropped on Hiroshima at 8.15 pm on August 6th 1945. 25th October 1945 saw the establishment of the United Nations – the fist global parliament. Its predecessor, the ineffectual League of Nations, founded in June 1919 at the time of the 'harsh and shortsighted treaty of Versailles', was swiftly forgotten.

Despite the 47 years of the Cold War a grudging peace prevailed in Europe and general affluence increased. And we are all familiar with the following scenario. Having lost its Empire, Britain rather uncertainly seeks a new role. Germany becomes a prosperous and model democracy. Japan embraces technology and accrues wealth second only to that of the United States. Totalitarian Communism collapses and Russia ceases to serve as a model for the very same section of the intelligentsia which had been so Russophile in the thirties. New and powerful economies emerge in Asia - China, Korea and, latterly, India – with a large and sophisticated computer software industry and a myriad web sites. South Africa becomes a black republic.

1972 saw World Cultures and Modern Art exhibition in Munich which was mounted to celebrate the XXth Olympiad.[19] The exhibition seemed hugely ambitious at the time, with its 2394 exhibits and its impressive World Music recitals. It would seem less remarkable today as we have become accustomed to living in a multicultural world. Nevertheless, this was the first exhibition to attempt to present artistic activity upon a global basis. It showed that the solipsistic view of Europe as the centre of all things was beginning to fade. The exhibition can be criticised retrospectively for the underlying assumption of its organisers of the ultimate superiority of European achievement. In the seventies 'Modern Art' could still be legitimately presented as the pinnacle of human artistic attainment. We have moved on.

The founding of The International Design Yearbook[20] in 1984 was evidence that design had become a global activity. The International Design Yearbook was born when international capitalism was in an assertive mood. Design became a profitable flavour-of-the-month add-on for entrepreneurs. Design offices, just like capital, are infinitely portable. Design, as it is usually presented to us, is a by-product of the highly capitalised industries which depend upon the constant acquisition of goods. A yearbook is by definition ephemeral. 'Today's good taste is tomorrow's hangover', said the American architect Robert Stern, the first editor of the *Yearbook*. Stern had established a considerable reputation with his vaudeville show classicism. His choice of designs for the first *Yearbook* still provides us with one of the most revealing records of postmodern taste at its apogée. Postmodernism, of course, was as international as the variegated sub-species of modernism which went before it. Furthermore, postmodernism represented an increasing awareness of historical and cultural pluralism. The guest editors of *The International Design Yearbook* were all almost household names – as far as designers ever can be.[21] All had formidable international reputations. Some countries, however, have gained reputations for excellence in design. Italy has produced a disproportionately high proportion of the designers represented in the *Yearbook* since 1985 – almost a quarter. Next, in descending order of representation comes Britain. Then follow Japan, Scandinavia (including Finland), Germany, the Netherlands, France and Switzerland. Design, as this suggests, is an activity confined to wealthy and highly industrialised nations. Wealth and power are presently concentrated within the hands of a few technologically advanced and powerful nations which dominate key industries. Ironically, the United States, the world's strongest industrial and economic power, has never been strongly represented in *The International Design Yearbook*.

The change that is now upon us is quite as momentous as the one which began with Gutenberg's invention of movable type at the end of the 15th century. The birth of a global consciousness is the most significant development since the beginning of the industrial age. We have learned that the German poet Heine was right when he declared that 'the axis of the earth projects in every town square'. We now know that Europe is such a town. But we are yet only barely conscious of the influence globalisation will have upon our communities, our micro and macro economies, our political lives. And, not least, upon the natural world. Is cultural diversity no more than a luxury – and even a potential cause of friction? Does globalisation necessarily mean Americanisation? Will the dominance of the English language prevent other modes of thinking from developing - mediated by different linguistic patterns? We speak six thousand different languages – how many will we be speaking in the year 2100? And what of our myriad metaphysical interpretations of the meaning of the cosmos?

The ability to diversify is one of humanity's supreme strengths. By an alchemy known in all cultures, we can transform the mundane into the transcendental. We mythologise, we recreate and we invent. Cultural diversity is surely as important to the well-being of our global psyche as bio-diversity is to our living environment. The world will become a barren place indeed if we all come to nourish our imaginations by the same homogenised theme parks – with their banal sentimentalisation of the past. Or subscribe to the trivialised versions of reality of the press. Or all watch similar mind-numbing television channels whose output is dictated only by rating figures. Is the process of globalisation controlling us? Or might we have a chance of controlling it?

Design can be no more than a palliative. The problems we face are too large to be amenable to the most intense efforts of designers. Designers can do little more than be useful. Consider the failure of the Modern Movement to transform society. Design can never change the world, although the world changes design readily enough.

But designers are frequently idealists. Designers will always be able to contribute to advancing the most worthy causes of humanity. Their sensibilities may help us to re-value what is good from the past. This may help to sustain us in the future.

Notes

1   The expression 'global village' was first used by Marshall McLuhan (1911-1980) in *The Gutenberg Galaxy. The making of typographic man*, Toronto, 1962. The book is not divided into conventional chapters and the term appears as an introduction to a short section headed : 'The new electronic interdependence recreates the world in the image of a global village'.

2   For the influence of non-Western architecture during the medieval period see : Bony, Jean, *The English Decorated Style. Gothic Architecture Transformed. The Wrightsman Lectures delivered under the Auspices of the New York University Institute of Fine Arts*, London, 1979. See pp. 23-5 for an account of the ogee. This is followed by 'Other Exotic Forms' which deals with Islamic influences upon medieval architecture. (pp. 25-6). Bony presents many excellent photographic illustrations to support his views. For an account of the early Italian borrowing of exotic motifs for textiles see : Santangelo, Antonino, *The Development of Italian Textile Design from the 12th to the 18th century*, London, 1964. See, in particular, Chapter I 'Twelfth Century Production : Islamic Influences at Palermo'. An example of a fourteenth century Venetian textile incorporating a recognisably Chinese dragon motif is illustrated in colour in plate 26.

3   See : Kruft, Hanno-Walter, *A History of Architectural Theory from Vitruvius to the Present*, London, 1994. See Chapter 1, 'Vitruvius and architectural theory in antiquity' and Chapter 2, 'The Vitruvian tradition and architectural theory in the Middle Ages'. 'Concrete interest in Vitruvius can be demonstrated only from Carolingian times, increasing in the High Middle Ages, and leading in the Renaissance to a degree of fame that Vitruvius can hardly have dreamt of.' Note 2, Chapter 2, contains a useful bibliography of accounts of the dissemination of Vitruvius's ideas.

4   William Jones (1746-94), was a judge in the service of the East India company. He was renowned throughout Europe for his knowledge of Oriental languages – Arabic, Hebrew, Persian and Sanskrit. He was also a very considerable scholar of Greek and Latin. He

became famous for his discovery of the close relationship between Sanskrit and Greek and Latin – he thought Sanskrit the most perfect of the three. The Abbé J A Dubois (1765-1848) went as a missionary to the Deccan (which includes what is now Tamilnadu) in 1792. He spent thirty-one years in India and learned Sanskrit and Tamil. He was the author of a number of works which were translated into English. The most famous of these is A *Description of the Character, Manners and Customs of the People of India* which appeared in many editions. He was also author of *Exposé de quelques-uns des principaux articles de la théogenie des Brahmes*, Paris, 1825 (An account of some of the principal aspects of the origins of the Gods according to the Brahmins) Isaac Titsingh was the author of *Illustrations of Japan; consisting of memoirs and anecdotes of the reigning dynasty of the Djogouns; a description of feasts and ceremonies "observed throughout the year at their court... remarks on their poetry; an explanation of their mode of reckoning time* Translated from the French. London, 1823. Titsingh's private correspondence has fairly recently been published in English.

5   Huxley, T. H. *Method and Results. Essays by Thomas H Huxley,* London, 1893, 'The Progress of Science 1837-1887', see pp. 42-3.

6   Max Nordau is a nom-de-plume. He was born Simon Maximilian Südfeld, the son of a rabbi, in Budapest. He drifted away from the Jewish community in his youth. Initially he worked as a journalist but later decided to study medicine. In 1880 his studies took him to Paris where he practised medicine for some time. He had a great interest in psychology and in the work of Jean-Martin Charcot (1825-93), a pioneering student of nervous and mental diseases - Freud was to be one of Charcot's students. It was as a controversial writer that Nordau was to make a name for himself. His first major work *Conventional Lies of Society* 1883   attacked irrationality and 'mysticism'. Such ideas were further developed in Degeneration 1895 – see following note. In the late 1890s – after meeting Theodor Herzl, the founder of modern Zionism and in the wake of rising anti-Semitism - Nordau became a fervent Zionist. It is as in this role that he is currently best known.

7   See Nordau, *Degeneration... Translated from the Second Edition of the German Work,* London, 1895. p. 39. The work is dedicated to Cesare Lombroso (1835-1909) 'dear and honoured master' who taught that criminality had a physiological basis. Lombroso's theory of atavism - regression to a primitive ancestral type - was attractive to middle class writers and readers, who feared a rising proletarian tide. Nordau's view of degeneration is described in his Dedication: 'Degenerates are not always criminals, prostitutes, anarchists, and pronounced lunatics; they are often authors and artists... Some among these degenerates in literature, music, and painting... are revered by numerous admirers as creators of a new art, and heralds of the coming centuries.' Nordau condemned the work of an extraordinary range of writers and artists including Aman-Jean, Kate Greenaway, Stéphane Mallarmé, Nietzsche, the Pre-Raphaelites – Rossetti in particular, Ruskin, every one of the Symbolists, Swinburne, Paul Verlaine – 'his face like a wicked angel grown old'.

8   These figures have been extrapolated from Nordau, op. cit. (see note 7). He lists the several sources from which his statistics are taken. 'In 1840 there were in Europe 3,000 kilometres of railway; in 1891 there were 218,000 kilometres. The number of travellers in 1840, in Germany, France and England, amounted to two and a half millions; in 1891 it was 614 millions. In Germany every inhabitant received, in 1840, 85 letters; in 1888, 200 letters. In 1840 the post distributed in France 94 millions of letters; in England, 277 millions; in 1881, 595 and 1,299 millions respectively. The collective postal intercourse between all countries, without including the internal postage of each separate country, amounted, in 1840, to 92 millions; in 1889, to 2,759 millions. In Germany, in 1840, 305 newspapers were published; in 1891, 6,800; in France, 776 and 5,182; in England (1846), 551 and 2,255. The German book trade produced, in 1840, 1,100 new works; in 1891, 18,700. The exports and imports

of the world had, in 1840, a value of 28, in 1889 of 74 thousand million marks. The ships which, in 1840, entered all the ports of Great Britain contained nine and a half, in 1890, seventy four and a half millions of tons. The whole British merchant navy measured, in 1840, 3,200,000; in 1890, 9,688,000 tons.'(p. 38.)

9   Among the more important international exhibitions were : The Great Exhibition of the Works of Industry of All Nations, London 1851; World's Fair of the Works of Industry of All Nations, New York 1853; Exposition Universelle, Paris 1855; International Exhibition, London 1862; International Exhibition of Arts and Manufactures, Dublin 1865; Exposition Universelle, Paris 1867; International Exhibitions, London – four exhibitions 1871, 1872, 1873 and 1874 (the project for mounting annual international exhibitions was not a success); Weltaustellung, Vienna 1873; International Exhibition of Philadelphia - the Centennial Exhibition – 1876; Exposition Universelle, Paris 1878; Exposition Coloniale d'Amsterdam 1883; Calcutta International Exhibition 1883–1884; The Colonial and Indian Exhibition London 1886; Exposició Universal, Barcelona 1888; Exposition Universelle Paris 1889; The World Columbian Exhibition, Chicago 1893; International Exhibition, Atlanta, Georgia 1895; Exposition Universelle, Paris 1900; Glasgow International Exhibition, 1901; Esposizione Internazionale d'Arte Decorativa Moderna, Turin 1902; The St Louis Exhibition 1904; Franco-British Exhibition, London 1908 (the remains of the exhibition are still to be found at Shepherd's Bush); Exposition Universelle et Internationale, Brussels 1910; The Japan-British Exhibition London 1910; Esposizione Internazionale d'Industria e di Lavoro, Turin 1911; Exposition Universelle et Industrielle, Ghent 1913; Deutschen Werkbund-Ausstellung Cöln, Cologne 1914 (although this was a specifically German exhibition – although there was an Austrian pavilion – the exhibition attracted so much international attention that it is included in this list); The Panama Pacific Universal Exposition, San Francisco 1915; Esposizione Triennale Internazionale delle Arti Decorative ed Industriali Moderne e dell'Architettura Moderna, Monza 1918 – this was a biennial exhibition which later moved to Milan; The British Empire Exhibition Wembley 1924; Exposition Internationale des Art Décoratifs et Industriels Modernes Paris 1925; Exposició Universal Barcelona 1929; Exposition Coloniale Internationale de Paris 1931; Exposition Universelle et Internationale de Bruxelles, Brussels 1935; A Century of Progress International Exhibition, Chicago 1933–34; Exposition Internationale des Arts at des Techniques appliqués à la vie moderne Paris 1937; British Empire Exhibition, Glasgow 1938; The World's Fair New York 1939–40; Golden Gate International Exposition, San Francisco 1939-40; Exposition Universelle 1et Internationale de Bruxelles. Expo'58, Brussels 1958; Century 21 Exposition, Seattle 1962; Universal and International Exhibition, Montreal. Expo '67, 1967; Japan World Exposition. Expo '70, Osaka 1970; Expo '92, Seville 1992.

10 The Exposition Universelle, which commemorated the centenary of the French Revolution, is probably the best documented of all the great international exhibitions. See Alphand, A,. *Exposition Universelle de 1889 à Paris*, Paris 1892; Dumas, F G and De Fourcaud, (eds.). *Revue de l'Exposition de 1889* (2 volumes), Paris 1889; Mathieu, Caroline (ed.). *La Tour Eiffel et l'Exposition Universelle*, Paris 1989 (catalogue of the centenary exhibition at the Musée d'Orsay); Monod, E. *L'Exposition Universelle de 1889. Grand Ouvrage Illustré. Historique, encyclopédique, descriptif. Publié sur le patronage de M. le Ministre du Commerce de l'Industrie et des Colonies* (4 volumes) Paris, 1890; Picard, Alfred(ed.). *Exposition Internationale de 1889 à Paris. Rapport General*, (10 volumes), Paris, 1891-2; Rousselet, Louis. *L'Exposition Universelle de 1889*, Paris, 1895, etc., etc..

11 In the wake of the success of the 1851 Exhibition, a Museum of Practical Art was set up in Marlborough House in 1852. The intention was to provide a didactic collection of the best in the applied arts for students as well as the public. In 1857 the collection was moved to South Kensington – the site of the present Victoria and Albert Museum – where it was

housed in a temporary structure clad in corrugated iron. (Nicknamed 'the Brompton Boilers'.) The museum was progressively extended until its completion in its present form in 1909.

12 See the following: *South Kensington Museum Art Handbooks*: China : Bushell, Stephen W. *Chinese Art* (2 volumes) London, 1904 ; India: Birdwood, G C M *The Industrial Arts of India* (2 volumes) London, 1884; The Islamic Countries: Lane-Poole, Stanley. *The Art of the Saracens in Egypt* (2 volumes) London, 1886; Smith, Major R. Murdoch, *Persian Art...* London, 1876; Japan: Franks, A. W. *Japanese Pottery*, being a native report. With an introduction and catalogue... with illustrations and marks, London, 1880. The South Kensington Museum also appears to have been the first institution to collect musical instruments on a global basis – see Engel, Carl. *Musical Instruments*, London, 1875.

13 See, for example: Christie, A. H. *Traditional Methods of Pattern Designing. An introduction to the study of decorative art*, Oxford, 1910, Crane, Walter. *The Bases of Design*, London, 1898; Day, Lewis F. *Ornament and its Application. A book for students treating in a practical way of the relation of design to material, tools and methods of work*, London, 1904; Glazier, Richard *A Manual of Historic Ornament treating upon the evolution, tradition and development of architecture and other applied arts. Prepared for the use of students*, London, 1899. There are very many other works which fall into this category.

14 The earliest attempt to reproduce photographs by printed means – as opposed to merely printing from negatives – was that of Fox Talbot in 1852. Then followed Paul Pretsch who devised a rival process in 1854. Both these processes were complex and time-consuming. Photogravure was invented by Karl Klic in 1879. By the end of the 1880 photogravure illustrations were appearing regularly in popular journals throughout Europe and America. (See Thomas, D. B. *The Science Museum Photography Collection*, London: HMSO 1969)

15 This list is taken from '*From today painting is dead*'. *The Beginnings of Photography* London, The Arts Council, 1972 – a catalogue of an exhibition at the Victoria and Albert Museum. See 'Collecting celebrities', cat. no 304.

16 See Fawcett, Trevor and Phillpot, Clive. *The Art Press. Two Centuries of Art Magazines. Essays published for the Art Libraries Society on the occasion of the International Conference on Art Periodicals and the exhibition The Art Press at the Victoria and Albert Museum, London*, London, 1976.

17 For example, Albert Speer's Grosse Halle project – a vast assembly hall for all the Germanic peoples. Its dome was to dominate Berlin. Begun in 1938, it was unfinished at Germany's defeat in 1945. Like other Nazi monuments, it was demolished.

18 Among the best known Italian modernists of the 1930s are Luciano Baldessari (1896–1982) – factory and exhibition design; Luigi Figini (1903–84) – who collaborated with Pollini in the design of the Olivetti industrial complex at Ivrea, Giovanni Michelucci (1891-1991) – the Santa Maria Novella Station in Florence; Gino Pollini (1903–91), Gino Ponti (1891–1979) – founder of the journal *Domus* and a prolific modernist architect, Mario Ridolfi (1904–84) – who was influenced by German moderns, including Gropius and Mendelsohn, (both of whom were discredited by the Nazis), and Giuseppe Terragni (1904–41) – the uncompromisingly modern Casa del Fascio, the Fascist headquarters at Como. Terragni is the most convincingly radical of the architects cited here. Italian modernism had particular local coloration, with 'rationalism' forming an important part of the agenda. The M.I.A.R. (Movimento Italiano per l'Architettura Razionale) was an important platform for architectural debate. Although the M.I.A.R. was forced to disband by the Fascists, modernist activity did not cease in Italy.

19 See *Weltkulturen und moderne Kunst. Die Beg{egnung der europäischen Kunst und Musik im 19. und 20. Jahrhunderts mit Asien, Afrika, Ozeanien, Afro- und Indo-Amerika. Ausstellung veranstaltet vom Organisationskomitee für der XX. Olympiade München 1972*, Munich, 1972. A digest of this 639 page catalogue was published in English as *World Cultures and Modern Art. The Encounter of 19th and 20th century European art and music with Asia, Africa, Oceania, Afro- and Indo-America. Exhibition on the occasion of the XXth Olympiad München 1972*, Munich, 1972.

20 *The International Design Yearbook* was published by Thames and Hudson between 1985-92. Later issues have been published by Laurence King & Co. The format of the book, which consists of about 240 pages with approximately 500 illustrations in colour of designs selected by the editor of the year, has changed little over the years. The following categories of design are represented: Furniture, Lighting, Tableware, Textiles, Products – bicycles, computers, digital cameras, electronic goods, kitchen gadgets, etc.

21 The editors of *The International Design Yearbook* have been: 1985/6 USA – Robert Stern; 1986/7 Argentina – Emilio Ambasz – born 1943; 1987/8 France – Philippe Starck – born 1949; 1988/9 Japan – Arata Isozaki – born 1931; 1989/90 Spain (Catalonia) – Oscar Tusquets Blanca – born 1941; 1990/91 Italy – Mario Bellini –born 1935; 1992 France – Andrée Putman – born 1925; 1993 Czechoslovakia –Borek Sipek – born 1949; 1994 Israel – Ron Arad – born 1951; 1995 France – Jean Nouvel – born 1945; 1996 Italy – Alessandro Mendini – born 1931; 1997 France – Philippe Starck; 1998 Germany – Richard Sapper – born 1932; 1999 Britain – Jasper Morison – born 1959.

interview with a designer on becoming designers

Richard Hill

Richard Hill is a designer for a multi-disciplinary company, Marketplace

The following is a short contribution arising from a conversation between Esther Dudley and Richard Hill, in which he outlines the characteristics needed by graduates, to become designers.

RH: Whatever else it is, becoming a designer is not a simple process and it certainly doesn't happen just because a university or college allows you to graduate from a design course. From that moment some focus is required and a clear agenda fixed in one's mind. I graduated in 1988 with a vague ambition to be a designer and watched others walk into great opportunities, those people being the ones who had a strong sense of purpose or just the knack of making the most of a lucky break. For the majority of us then, as now, the lucky break had to be earned over a period of time.

ED: How can you ensure that the chance will come?

RH: You have to make it happen by showing what it is that motivates you. You want to be different and find a channel for creativity that marks you from the crowd. Steve Jobs at Apple claims that his company creates opportunities for designers to deliver astounding visions, by nurturing the 'crazies'. The most important characteristics, I would argue, are passion, self-belief and awareness of the broader picture. The late Tibor Kalman said, 'Good artists make trouble.' This also applies to designers. There is little point in going through an expensive education simply to graduate with the same ideas as 49,999 others. The designers I admire and respect are the people who stand for something. We don't need to be anarchic or confrontational for the sake of being awkward. But we should challenge the monopolies, champion the vulnerable and ask lots of questions.

I believe that few design companies would want to employ designers simply to replicate work that they are already identified with. The productive partnership has to have the dynamics that come from being passionate about design. Obviously when there are at least two viewpoints, the atmosphere can be confrontational, exciting and uncertain. Yet certainty is the territory of the marketeer, not the designer.

ED: What difference can the client make to the way you work?

RH: The best results come from the chemistry between a client who has a powerful vision and the designer who can understand that vision and apply real creativity to it. Sometimes the client can mistake an individual, who refuses to accept things at face value, as 'difficult'. Well occasionally it is our job to be difficult, to bring about a more creative solution.

ED: What practical advice do you have for graduates who are about to go into the profession?

RH: Really good designers are polymaths. Knowing about typography, for instance, isn't a simple case of recognising the names of 3000 (5000, 8000?) forms of font and face. Typography is also about culture and cultures; markets and marketing; form and function; age and demographics; media and message. Understanding the world (or attempting to) leads to better, different, exuberant and passionate typography. At first you will be a pretty small fish. That is your advantage, as you have little to lose. Build your profile through the ubiquitous portfolio. For an interview, make sure you represent your real interests. If you are really into music, place your work in CD cases or 12" record sleeves and don't be afraid to rave about the stuff you like. It shows you care about something. For designer, think catalyst, visual champion, trouble-maker or anything that opens up possibilities. Possibilities are everything.

'ethical design': the end of graphic design?

Alex Cameron

Alex Cameron is co-director of the design consultancy, Cameron Sedley. Cameron Sedley produce an artspaper, Caffeine, edited by Richard Sedley, and have organised debates and conferences on art and design including New Design (Institute of Contemporary Art, July 1998), Gridlocked?: Contemporary Graphic Design and In conversation with Ken Garland (Riverside Studios, London, March 1999), and Crosscurrents (Exeter Phoenix, March 1999).

Introduction

When should you shut-up and let people have their own say? In *Amistad*, the Spielberg blockbuster, slave mutineers stand trial in the New Republic, that we now know as the USA. The defendants, speaking no English, are appointed an African-born and English-speaking former slave to act as their translator.

The mutineers' defence that they were 'free born Africans', not slaves, was deeply problematic for a government fearing the reaction of the southern states to the notion of a free-born black man that could not be legally enslaved.

In the courtroom sat the defendants' judges. But an important addition to the usual players was the translator. The court would ask the questions through the translator to the defendants and vice versa. What a wonderful place to be! To be part of a process of communicating between men from different parts of the world and to enable one of the great discussions of freedom to take place.

As the courtroom drama unfolded and passions inflated, damning and irrational accusations were levelled at the defendants, such that instead of waiting for a response the translator screamed his own defence of those in the dock. I imagine that if I found myself in that place, I too may have shouted back. It was an emotional act based on his understanding of what is right and wrong.

But the translator was wrong. His attachment to the cause of justice for his people,undermined actual justice because justice dictates that people should choose their own defence and have their own say. The translator 'broke the rules' by momentarily acting not as translator, as facilitator, but as judge and jury.

New Britain, new design

In New Labour's New Britain naturally we have New Design. New Design, a term coined by Kevin McCullagh of the radical Design Agenda group, aptly draws attention to the way that broader ideological currents are gaining influence among leading designers, journalists and design institutions.

While there has been some *critical* discussion of the New Labour phenomenon, it strikes me that there has been precious little critical discussion of these trends among graphic designers. Ideas have entered into the mindset of many practitioners without much reaction, most explicitly in the form of ethical design.

The ethical designer is the New Man of the New Design world. Ethical design demands of its practitioners that they question the content of any project. In this view, the content of a project is the yardstick by which work is measured. The moral and ethical qualities should determine whether that project or idea should be afforded the designer's time.

The ethical trend in design thinking has far-reaching consequences for the practice, and perception, of the role of the graphic designer and indeed the design industry. The result of bringing ethics into design is potentially damaging for all concerned.

My questioning of ethics might seem odd. After all, who wants to be unethical? One's ethics – according to the dictionary, one's moral philosophy or moral principles – should surely guide one's life.

However, it is my contention that in the case of design one must be true to others to be true to oneself. The principle of the designer as mediator should remain the baseline of our profession.

Design has existed for a long time without the concept of ethical design. Graphic design has flourished with a more commonsense understanding of the role of the graphic designer and graphic design in society. For design to advance in any meaningful, practical, creative and lasting sense, practitioners have to be true to their craft.

The designer as mediator, an uncontroversial idea hitherto, is in the firing line in the form of the promotion of a new model designer, fit for the new millennium, the 'ethical designer'. No longer should the designer be allowed to see himself as an effective transmitter of ideas and information but he must now rise up and challenge the content of the message. It is a current in graphic design that, for those interested in designs future, cannot be ignored.

Ethical design is the modern son of green design. Many questioned green design on its emergence in the mid-eighties, as the applicability of environmentalism to many areas of design was not apparent (a green typeface?). In other areas such as product design there had been an unceasing attempt to make more efficient use of resources, so what's new? Ethical design, unlike its less subtle predecessor, targets not so much the practicalities of design itself but more insidiously the outlook behind design.

143

Perhaps crudely we can say that while green design coincided with misgivings about industrial society and development, ethical design dovetails with the even deeper disenchantments in the nineties. This time disenchantment with organisations, institutions, politicians and even politics in general. Throughout the eighties and nineties traditional institutions, methods of political action and protest have been undermined to the extent that the certainties of the past seem to have all but disappeared.[2,4,12,14,15,16] These changes have had a profound effect on policy-making in government and decision-making in the boardroom but they have also called into question design thinking.

Ethical design in some sense is a response to a sense of political powerlessness: designers are urged to get off the fence and act. But what does it mean when design is accorded this role in the world?

The loss of design and art direction

The American Institute of Graphic Arts 'Dangerous Ideas' conference in the USA, at the end of the eighties, was something of a landmark in changing the parameters in which design and advertising are discussed. The late Tibor Kalman and co-chair Milton Glaser raised moral and ethical issues within the design industry that kick-started a discussion within graphic design about where the designer was situated in the broader context of a changing social and political landscape.

Kalman's starting point was an attempt to make designers face up to the seeming contradictions within graphic design. From 'making the filthy oil company look "clean"' to 'making the junky condo look "hip"'.[9]

In the early nineties Cranbrook Academy of Art's Katherine McCoy took Kalman's ethical dilemma further when she put it as a choice between 'client or content'.[7] In other words, if you don't like the content, ditch the client. By 1993, according to McCoy, the designers who chose the client were acting not unlike the prostitute who provides a service that demands they remain unattached and neutral.[13] While no doubt most designers have indeed felt like prostitutes at one time by another, selling themselves to somebody they dislike, McCoy's couplet is little more than an intellectual sleight of hand that disguises an attack on the professionalism and profession of the designer.

Throughout the nineties the ethical bandwagon rolled on through design schools and design publications such as Cranbrook Academy of Arts in the USA and the British based *Eye*, the international review of graphic design, to name a few.

In early 1999 Kalle Lasn, founding editor of the North American environmentalist/anti-consumerist *Adbusters* magazine, took the ethical proposition to its logical conclusion, at a talk at the Royal College of Art's *Points of View* series in London, when he compared the 'unethical' graphic designer to the SS guards at the gates of Auschwitz. The logic of the argument is clear: designers are responsible for all the problems in society, from children smoking to animal testing, nuclear power and war.

Lasn announced that they were rewriting British designer and author Ken Garland's key 1964 *First Things First* design manifesto. By the end of the summer of 1999, the new manifesto *First Things First 2000* (FTF2000) had been published in seven magazines: *Adbusters* in Canada, *Emigre* and the *AIGA Journal* in the USA, *Eye* and *Blueprint* in London, *Items* in the Netherlands and *Form* in Germany.

The design ethics proposed by the signatories of FTF2000 is at best a call foɪ designers to 'design for good' and at worst is a prescriptive set of moral codes. While the prescriptive nature of ethical design is apparent, it is often presented as a matter of choice.

However, the very idea of the use of ethics presented in the new manifesto makes two assumptions about design and its practice that are fundamentally flawed and dangerous: that graphic design can play a determining role in how people think and act and that the 'end-user' or consumer is powerless and therefore unable to resist.

Design as social engineering

The election of New Labour to government had an almost immediate impact on the design industry in Britain. A debate raged soon after, following on from a discussion document by the think-tank Demos on the perceptions of Britain at home and abroad,[11] a document that was greeted with derision [1,6,10] as much as with excitement.

Design consultancy Wolff Ollins released some sketches of what the new British flag would look like were the decision taken to bury the Union Flag, with all its associations with Empire and Britain's racist past.

Further discussions raged about how the perception and the seeming reality of Britain could be put right through design. Proposals that have all but been pushed under the carpet were bounced around, from taking foreign delegates to the Ministry of Sound rather than the Tower of London to the positive promotion of Britain as a centre of creative service-providers as opposed to the perception of Britain as a declining manufacturing nation.

Can the designer change Britain's image? The problem was and remains that peoples' perceptions of Britain as a declining power have such currency because it is. A sea change in perception demands a sea change in what is in fact happening. Only with the reorganisation of British society and industry could graphic designers play their part. Without it there is little to spin. Designers would do well to explain that design is at its most effective when it draws on the pre-existing prejudices and beliefs and hopes and fears of the consumer or end-user.

Another example of the attempt to implicate design in social change is the legislation banning the advertising of cigarettes in public places. The argument here is that stopping the wicked drug barons using the images of purple silk will stop people smoking and thus improve the nation's health. Again, the assumption is that design can have a determining influence on how people act. The resounding silence from the design industry on this question should allow us to assume that the industry believes that advertising makes people smoke. But as recent history has shown, just as many people start smoking today as they did 30 years ago and that is with the continual restriction of where and how tobacco can be advertised. In general, teenagers start smoking because they see it as a quick step into adult life. For a 13 year old this is a more 'sexy' proposition than a peeling roadside billboard, passed on the way home from school.

The right to choose

An understanding of the impact of 'design' in society is necessary in order to develop it further, as well as to allow those who practise to concentrate on their overriding responsibility: to communicate the ideas they are given in as effective a manner as possible. Effective communication, raising the standards of design and its practice enables the consumer to exercise greater choice.

For ethical designers choice has become a dirty word. Their concern is that if we allow people the choice between a 'good' product and a 'bad' product people may choose the 'bad' one. This is the logic of the censor, the 'old lefts' argument that "no platform" should be given to those beyond the pale, such as fascists and anti-abortion groups.

During my time at college, student activists would often chant "no platform" throughout a debate or, worse, call in the authorities to ban the debate on the spurious grounds of public disorder. Their argument, like that of today's ethical designer, was that things they disliked (a lot) should not be expressed. In part this showed a fear that they were unable to argue their case against people such as anti-abortionists, but in main the view was that the audience were like sheep. Under no circumstances could people be trusted to hear such dangerous ideas.

Desperately disillusioned with their fellow man, the ethical designer wants no choice of competing products or ideas to be presented. When choice is a dirty word then what does that say about the consumer?

Taking the influence of advertising to the absurd, as is evident in the writings of ethical designers, an image is conjured up where consumers are unable to view advertising without getting on the telephone to order the 'vacumeasy' or the "staysharp cutlery". Having managed to turn-off the TV we only have to walk ten feet before we are persuaded to buy an alternative brand of cigarettes while at the same time being coerced into buying some perfume that we glimpsed out of the corner of our eye on the back page of an upturned magazine.

Choice is only possible if we retain a certain level of critical faculties. Choice is relevant only to those who are able to exercise that choice. It presumes a fundamental belief in human agency. It is this rejection of human agency that sets the ethical designer apart from all who came before.

What is happening is that the ethical designer takes design both too seriously and not seriously enough. By assuming that the world spins around design, the ethicist treats design too seriously. By concentrating on the content of the message, rather than on how best to get the message across, the ethicist does not treat the craft of design seriously enough.

Both taking design too seriously and not seriously enough shows a low view of people. On the one hand people are sheep who will believe what they are shown and, on the other, not intelligent enough to warrant someone who concentrates his skill and effort in the process of effectively getting ideas across.

What is the role of the graphic designer?

At the heart of the ethical problem is its prescriptive nature. At the outset we should recognise that this is not a question of a 'preferred way of working' nor indeed is it an enlightened next step in the progressive and developmental nature of graphic design.

I would argue that the demand for designers to be ethical is a demand for an end to designer as mediator as we know it.

The demand for an ethical graphic design industry is rooted in the near total collapse of many of the old institutes that were the product of the expansion of the industry during the 1950s and 60s. Like many other post war institutions, they have suffered in the face of a changing social and political landscape.

From the rejection of the old, a new set of standards and goals are being reformulated. While we should not necessarily simply reintroduce the ideas of the past, we should certainly be wary of throwing the proverbial baby out with the bathwater.

Few would doubt the need for a more critical and robust review of the role of the graphic designer. The industry is constantly evolving and we would do well to keep up with developments in the fields of theory, practice and technology.

Fundamentally, we need to examine what the role of the graphic designer is, both for the purposes of review and for our standard of practice. We would do no harm in having this debate in public as it would show the depth of understanding within the industry and introduce the practices and workings of our industry to a broader audience.

At the outset, the graphic designer is a problem-solver. The problem to solve is how best to communicate the message that is given, to those identified as likely to use the service. The message can be anything from telling people the price of a fast car and where to get it, to a more challenging problem of how to get people from A to B in a hospital or an airport. In both instances an unwritten contract is agreed: that the designer will draw on all their experience, skill and expertise to mediate that message visually, to those who need or want that information. Again, in both cases, we should assume that the easier the message (or the more effective in design terms) is to understand (the what, the where and the how), the better.

The challenge is set and the designer is employed to mediate that message at his or her discretion. Importantly, this relationship or contract recognises the expertise of the graphic designer. It recognises the designer as central to the communication process.

But, perhaps, more importantly as designers we must understand that the people for whom the product is targeted are discerning individuals who are able to make choices, presuming they are given one!

The ethical designer turns this relationship on its head. The content of the message is questioned, on personal (do I believe in / agree with the content) and moral grounds (does the message promote 'unethical' signs). The role of the graphic designer becomes one of a moral guardian.

While there is, of course, nothing wrong with choosing not to work for a client based on one's own personal opinion, or beliefs, we must make a distinction between what is a personal decision and what is by its nature a prescriptive set of demands on designers and the design industry. A cursory review of the ethical question in graphic design reveals that the concerns of designers are of course a reflection of the general concerns of society, based on an irrational fear of the unknown.[3]

A vox pop in *Graphics International* magazine asked creatives to comment on their companies' ethical concerns about vivisection. In other discussions you are likely to find these themes repeated with additions like the defence industry, cars and recently GM foods.[5]

There is often a broad consensus on these ethical concerns. But, thankfully, ideas are still contested. That there is a general attack on the production of GM foods does not mean the attackers are right. Let Monsanto have its say! Similarly 'animal testing' has its critics as well as its proponents. The point being that the graphic designer is not responsible for society's beliefs and prejudices and as a mediator is limited to repeating or ignoring them, based on the interests of the originator.

In his introduction to *Graphic Design: A Concise History*, Richard Hollis says of the role of the graphic designer, 'The meaning that images and alphabetic signs convey has little to do with who made or chose them: they do not express their designers' ideas. The designer's message serves the expressed needs of the client who is paying for it. Although its form may be determined or modified by the designer's aesthetic preferences or prejudice, the message has to be put in a language recognised and understood by its intended audience.'[8]

The 'designer as mediator' is a principle that we would do well to defend.

References/bibliography

1   Bayley, S. *Labour Camp: The Failure of Style over Substance*, Batsford 1998

2   Fukuyama, F. *The End of History*, Peguin 1995

3   Furedi, F. *Culture of Fear: Risk-taking and the Morality of Low Expectation*, Cassell 1997

4   Giddens, A. *Beyond Left and Right*, Polity 1995

5   Graphics International magazine, October 1997

6   Heartfield, J. LM magazine, November 1997

7   Heller, S (ed.). *Design Dialogues* Allworth Press 1998

8   Hollis, R. *Graphic Design: A Concise History* Thames and Hudson 1994

9   Hall, P. and Bierut, M. (eds.). *Tibor Kalman: Perverse Optimist*, Booth–Clibborm 1998

10 Kirkpatrick, J. Speech at New Design conference, London 1998

11 Leonard, M. *Rebranding Britain: Renewing Our Identity*, Demos 1997

12 Mandelson, P. *The Blair Revolution* 1996

13 McCoy, K. *Design Renaissance: Selected Papers from the International Design Congress*, Open Eye Publishing 1993

14 Real World Coalition, *The Politics of the Real World*, Earthscan 1996

15 Whiteley, P. and Seyd, P. (eds.). *Labour Grass Roots* Clarendon Press 1995

16 Whiteley, P., Seyd, P. and Richardson, J. (eds.). *True Blues: The Politics of Conservative Party Membership*, Clarendon Press 1995

towards more ambitious agendas

Gerard Mermoz

Gerard Mermoz was educated at the Faculte des Lettres et Sciences Humaines d'Aix-en-Provence, where he studied Literature and Art History. He later studied design history and theory at Bristol University, then at Liverpool Polytechnic. His research focused on semiological aspects of art, design and communication from a multidisciplinary perspective and was published in Art History, Novum, IDEA and the acts of the Brno biennale. In 1991 he developed an interest in typography and has since taught, experimented and contributed to the debate on the 'new typographies', notably in EMIGRE, Baseline and Visible Language. His interests span a wide range of visual practices; from collage to sound and electronic media. His current work focuses on the relation between language, typography and sound. He is currently principal lecturer in typography at the University of the West of England, in Bristol.

One ambitious role for graphic design education today is to develop a realistic and functional balance between the respective needs and capabilities of the author, the text, the image, the medium, the platform (print, CD Rom, www, etc.), the message, the client, the audience, the design profession, the design language and, finally, what we might call, generically, society at large. This will entail focusing our attention and our responsibilities more specifically onto the fields of Semiotics, Ethics and Aesthetics.

Although I take it as read that certain obvious objectives need to be pursued, such as to equip students with appropriate tools and attitudes for a professional life as designers, provide appropriate supports for users of graphic communication (industry, public services, individuals, etc.) and keep up with technological and other developments, I believe that graphic design education (as distinguished from vocational training) should be more intellectually and artistically ambitious and be the place where new agendas should be set for graphic design and designers, beyond the commercial needs and concerns of industry.

This will entail developing new pedagogic frameworks in which appropriate ranges of skills and knowledge will be cultivated and shared by staff and students, in a spirit of purposeful experimentation.

I shall begin my discussion by insisting on the need to transcend certain ideological conflicts within the graphic profession; conflicts which, by emphasizing polemics rather than critical enquiry, have prevented graphic design from developing more artistically and intellectually ambitious forms of expressions, beyond superficial styling exercises or dutiful communications of information.

I have structured my essay in five sections, which outline a specific set of requirements.

Ideological conflicts: the situation now... and how we might resituate and redefine graphic design on the basis on a healthy pluralism

As recent international debates in *Eye, Emigré* and *Print* magazine testify, the graphic design community has been – and still is – divided by fundamental differences concerning the nature of the discipline and its role in society. On one side, stand the promoters of hedonistic consumption and life style, who claim to engage in free experimentation and self-expression; on the other stand those who view design as a public service and argue that the designer should serve the author and not interfere with the message.

This fundamental divide, particularly apparent in typography, has been un-necessarily exacerbated by oversimplistic references to the concepts of Modernism and Postmodernism; as if the plurality of approaches and interventions available to us could be neatly fitted into one or the other category, and as if the two categories were mutually exclusive. Although I believe that clearly enunciated principles can be useful to focus on issues, I also believe that they can be counter-productive when used as universal, non-negotiable truths. This is why I prefer to see design work as a working through of hypotheses.

My suggestion here is that the ideological content and dimension of design practice should not only be acknowledged but examined in relation to criteria of appropriateness. For the question here is not to determine which ideology (modernism or postmodernism) is right and deserves promoting across the design arena but, more pertinently, 'is the practice effective in implementing its aims and is it in keeping with other requirements? (not just those of the client, or of the intended audience, but ethical ones as well – what I encompassed, earlier, under the category of the social).

This will necessarily mean extending the view of the designer's role beyond the generic formulation of 'helping the client sell his or her product' and considering, more specifically, what design actually contributes to the communication process, how it implements its effects on its intended audiences, and, finally, considering its wider implications (social, cultural, political, semiological, etc.). The recent instance, when Saatchi & Saatchi were accused by Gillian Wearing' of having stolen her artistic idea/property and turned it into a commercial, provides a useful example for discussion concerning the relation between fine art and design practices.

Personally, I would argue that paying greater attention to the multifunctionalities of design is a more productive way of resolving ideological differences, since different contexts call for different solutions which, in turn, call for different combinations of functions (Mermoz, 1995). To adopt and promote a narrow, static aesthetic stance and to assume that it could be of universal value for graphic design in general is too simplistic; we must learn to live, work and enjoy life in multicultural and multifunctional environments. And by this I don't mean that designers should just learn to tolerate each other but, more importantly, try and appreciate the wider variety of options currently on offer and thus become multilingual and culturally multifaceted, as well as multi-task performers.

Unlocking the present stalemate and opening up dialogue, in a spirit of mutual respect and understanding, should be an essential priority of design education if it is to rise to the challenges that graphic design already has to face in the wake of recent technological develoments, changing social and economic conditions and, simultaneously, the effect of globalisation and the extension of cultural pluralism.

153

That education institutions should take initiatives in this domain was made painfully obvious by a recent seminar I attended at the ICA, in London where a panel of designers, asked to comment on the challenges brought about by new technologies, proved unable to offer any real insights beyond reiterating the most obvious clichés such as 'we must attend to an increased number of tasks previously shared with printers and type setters', 'our chief duty is to our clients' or 'we must use our new tools creatively', etc. What stood out, for me, was that the crucial challenge brought about by new technologies, in terms of new forms of collaborative authorship (a fast developing area of fine art practice –combined arts) was not even identified, let alone discussed, even when the issue was raised from the floor.

Looking beyond our borders

We can learn from the United States and countries of Europe such as France, Holland and Germany, where a higher level of debate has taken place. For in Britain, with the notable exception of EYE magazine, the level of debate is struggling to rise above that of listing journalism and seems unable or unwilling to venture into the more stimulating route of detailed analyses and issue-based discussions. As Rick Poynor[12] points out in a recent issue of EYE, our discipline is poorly served by the publishing industry, which seems content to publish glossy annuals and coffee table anthologies; it is also plagued by a low level of debate within the profession, with a few notable exceptions.

It is significant that a few years ago at a conference in Manchester debating the future of multimedia education, TOMATO refused to respond to the agenda set by the organizers, insisting that they would only present their showreel on their own terms.

In France a few years ago, graphic designers met to elaborate and discuss a charter which would provide guidelines for professional practice (in which the ethical and philosophical implications of specific graphic practices were highlighted rather than brushed under the carpet).

To argue that rethinking what graphic design is and does is an important aspect of education's role has serious implications about the curriculum: in particular on what and how we teach. Not just about the course content (what blend should be achieved between technical, conceptual and cultural components) but about the range of methodologies we should bring to bear on the subject – when formulating problems, hypothesis and elaborating solutions; when analysing, 'criting' and discussing works; when considering the wider implications of our choices and how we might plan and run our partnerships with industry; how flexibly we might define the professional options at undergraduate and postgraduate levels.

Put concretely, this means not merely setting projects which simulate those of industry (such as designing a brochure, a poster or a website), but chosing projects which enable staff and students to raise and discuss issues, focus on specific design parameters and consider the implications of design choices, beyond questions of personal tastes.

Integrating diversity on an enlarged functional basis

Issue 47 of EMIGRE, entitled 'relocating design' (1998) identified constraints and polarities within design, with contributions by Loraine Wild, Jeff Keedy, Michael Shea and Rudy VanderLans.

Noting that the problem, for us, is 'how to salvage graphic design in the face of the juggernaut of technology and the demands of the market' (a formulation which echoes VanderLans's editorial), Loraine Wilds suggested: 'to nurture authentic individual voices in graphic design, and to recognize that individuality manifests itself in form made independently of conceptual analysis or the market', which led her to argue for greater emphasis on the making process and a re-evaluation of craft skills in an experimental perspective.[7]

This echo of Barthes's invitation to the Pleasure of the Text is hardly new stuff, and I very much doubt if playing down conceptual analysis might help designers – or design – escape from the pressures of markets and technology; for acknowledging the creative part (which part/s?) played by concepts in design should not rule out – nor play down – the contribution of other factors, such as intuition, engagement with form and material, improvisation, etc. What we need, rather, is a way of integrating all these factors and showing how they might operate within a flexible structure, in dynamic relationships with each other.

It is unfortunate that the term 'concept' should feature in the article as a demonized cliché, within an either/or position: 'is graphic design only a conceptual process?' asks Wild; but this is a clumsy way of posing (and then answering) the question. What should be at issue is not whether graphic design should be conceptual or formal but rather to reach a better undestanding of how form and concepts might be made to interact and take effect in purposeful designs; and to show how, when form seems to guide the process, concepts are quietly working in the background, less rigidly than normally assumed, until the 'eureka' phase produces the final insight.

To put it simply, I would say that what we need is greater sophistication in our understanding of how graphic design works. Translated into pedagogic practice, this means paying close attention to the parameters of design and investigating how specific design structures can generate specific perceptual effects, within limits of probability.

The graphic designer as (freewheeling) semiologist

What follows from the above is that the graphic designer needs to turn semiologist (in a freewheeling Barthesian sense – not in a stuffy academic one; i.e. one which might cancel out the usefulness of semiological concepts/tools under a barrier of jargon). This requirement is closely linked with a need for a design poetics.[1]

Since every artistic practice involves specific, purposeful action onto specific parameters, normally within, and sometimes against acknowledged paradigms, graphic design education must extend its references to other disciplines and methodologies if graphic design is to fulfil the increasingly varied and complex tasks it is called upon to fulfil (not just the styling of magazines but the reinterpretation of old genres – the book is not dead! – and the development of new ones, either for print or digital platforms). Since unanalysed problems are not likely to receive effective solutions, analytical skills must be developed to conceptualise the problems, identify possible solutions and test their effectiveness. But this must not be at the expense of other, more intuitive, modes of approach.

At a time when the aesthetic and expressive functions of graphic communication are increasingly interpreted in narrow (regressive and narcissistic) terms, it is also important to rediscover the full scope of visual–conceptual–intuitive–creative intervention available to us through the design continuum.

Cross-disciplinary path: from literature to multimedia

That a debate between Proust and Ruskin about the nature of reading might be introduced in the presentation of a piece of multimedia about experimental typography[10] is a reminder that fundamental processes such as reading and the interpretation of meanings apply across a diversity of media and platforms (print or screen). The skill, with the development of new technologies, will be to subtly integrate knowledge from different disciplines according to criteria of relevance and appropriateness. This will mean not confusing texts (as strategies for representing alternative worlds in language) with texts as quantities of printed matter (the text blocks of DTP packages). Much nonsense about the 'death of the book' rests on such confusions.

The paradox is that, outside the area of display and advertising – where persuasion calls for, and is achieved through, emphatic forms of visual rhetoric – graphic and typographic communication at large operates at conceptual levels which are not immediately accessible by looking. In an article entitled 'Deconstruction and the Typography of Books' (1998), I have shown a propos of deconstructive texts how typography is not a visual intervention on the appearance of a text but a conceptual-visual interpretation of the strategies of the text. Failing to understanding this fact, certain commentators have called 'deconstructive' the superficial dressing up or optical blurring of otherwise perfectly traditional texts. Duchamp's critique of retinal art bears relevance here, especialy at a time when superficial optical values are enjoying a revival – through virtual reality – and presented as avant-garde and progressive.

To conclude

The challenge and responsibility of redefining and extending the theoretical basis of graphic design calls for the development of more theoretically ambitious pure and applied research programmes within graphic design education and the selective and strategic integration of their findings in the curriculum.

This means extending our concerns beyond the limited horizon of passing fashions into the realm of visual language, pleasure (of the image, the text, sound and their interaction), communication, far-reaching experimentation, engage-ment with form, ideas, recognizing and assuming our responsibilities as communicators and 'form-givers'.

Research is particularly urgent in the following areas: the nature of graphic communication, in particular the study of the interaction between different elements, parameters and values and their effects on specific audiences, within particular forms of expression; and what we may generically refer to as visual language, the relation between technology and its creative application in design (against the too facile technocentric approaches which, paradoxically, encourage too literal applications of software and the proliferation of ready-made effects.

On the Digital Media MA course at the University of the West of England, in Bristol, fine art, typography, film language, narrative structures, theories of meaning and experimental sound and music provide useful reference points and methodological tools to explore and develop new design possibilities and design strategies for CD-Rom, websites or multimedia installations, all in a spirit of purposeful experimentation.

157

Researching in this multi-and cross-disciplinary vein, I am currently working on the theme 'for a typography of the voice', in an attempt to explore the relation between the phonic and the semantic. The first outcome of this research was presented at the annual conference of the French society of typographers in the form of a multimedia performance, with the French trombone player Thierry Madiot. The project brings together Barthes (Empire of Signs; The Grain of the Voice), Joyce (Ulysses, chapter of the Sirens), Cage [Roatorio], Luciano Berio

(Thema: omaggio a Joyce, Sequenza III, Visage), Derrida (Cinders and Glas), Attik Design [Noise], experimental Jazz groups from France, Italy, Holland and Britain, and more, to be identified, montaged and edited in the form of a polylogue: a multiplicity of voices which, by a series of individual propositions, invite us to rethink the relations between the notions of author, text, reader, creation, meaning and interpretation.

After the sensory delight and/or intellectual challenge and stimulus induced by these experiments, I have no doubt that renewed resources of energy and enthusiasm will be found at the time when more prosaic tasks are to be performed and deadlines met. Such is the effect and value of pure experimentation, for a discipline which cannot – and should not – forget the difference between constraints, freedom and responsibilities.

Selected Readings

1   Baker S. *To go about noisily: Clutter, writing and design*, Emigré, no. 35, 1995

2   Blauvelt A. (ed.). *Critical Histories of Graphic Design*, Visible Language, no. 28.3,4, 1994 and 29.1, 1995

3   Burdick A. (ed.). *Mouthpiece, collection of new writings about graphic design*, Emigré, nos. 35-6, 1995

4   *Deconstruction and the Typography of Books*, Baseline, no. 25, 1998 p.41-4

5   *Design Writing Research, writing on graphic design*, London: Phaidon 1996

6   Emigré nos. 33-51 (an important site of critical debate about graphic design)

7   Emigré no. 47:19, 1998

8   Friedman D. *Radical Modernism*, New Haven and London: Yale University Press, 1994

9   Lupton E. & Abbott Miller J. *The abc's of triangle, square and circle: the bauhaus and design theory*, London: Thames & Hudson 1993

10 Mermoz G. *On Typographic Reference*: part one, EMIGRE, no. 36, 1995

11 Poynor R. *Design without Boundaries*, London Booth-Clibborn 1998

12 Poynor R. *Publishing by numbers*, EYE, vol. 8, Spring 1999 p.6-7

13 Duis L. and Haase A.*The World Must Change: graphic design and idealism*, Sandberg Institut 1999

14 The '*Body of the Text*': Typographic Interface and Interactive Reading, paper published in the Acts of the Symposium Interface 3: 'Labile Ordnungen', Hamburg, 1996 p.188-198

15 van Toorn J. (ed.). *Design Beyond Design, a critical reflection and the practice of visual communication*, Leyden Jan van Eyck Akademie 1998.